CW00404778

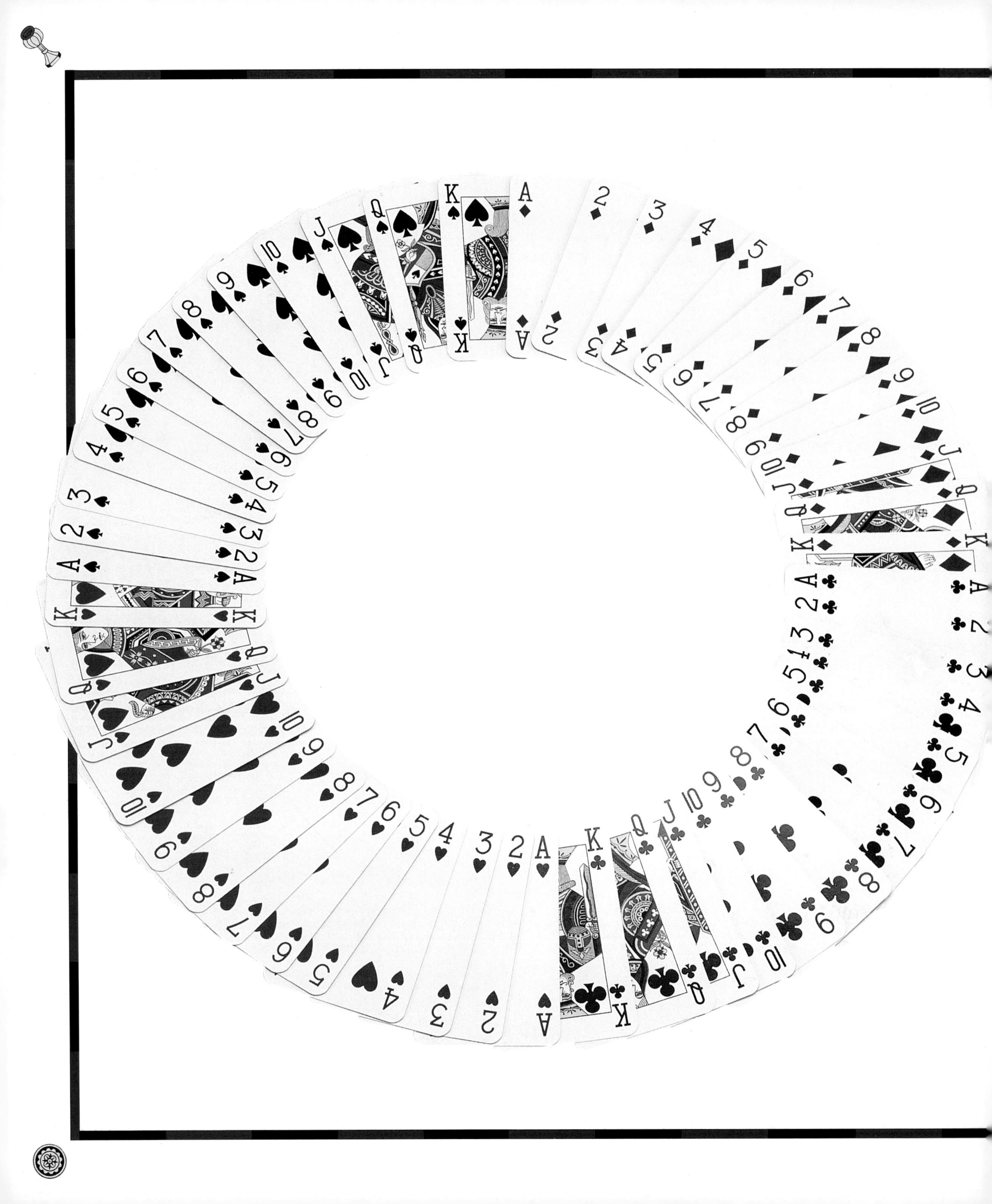

TAROT AND CARD PREDICTION

DISCOVER HOW CARDS CAN HELP YOU TO DIVINE THE FUTURE

JOAN MOORE

TIGER BOOKS INTERNATIONAL
LONDON

To my husband Denys, who was, is and always will be . . .

The Tarot deck used in the majority of the photographs illustrating this book is the Ancien Tarot de Marseille deck. It is reproduced here with the kind authorization of its publisher:
Frances Cartes,
BP 49,
54130 Saint Max,
France

To the memory of Taliesin III – shaman, mystic and intuitive exponent of the cards.

CLB 4066

This edition published in 1995 by Tiger Books International plc, Twickenham

ISBN 1-85501-769-5

Picture Credits
The publishers would like to thank both the Bridgeman Art Library and Images Colour Library for supplying the following illustrations for the book:
The Bridgeman Art Library: 68TR (Bibliothèque Nationale, Paris), 68L (Christopher Wood Gallery, London), 69L (Giraudon/ Musée de la Ville de Paris, Musée Carnavalet), 69TR (Blenheim Palace, Oxon), 70B (Giraudon/ Louvre Museum, Paris), 80-1 (Christie's, London), 81TL (Giraudon/Musée de la Chartreuse, Douai), 88 (King Street Galleries, London), 104 (Stapleton Collection).
Images Colour Library: 10BL, 11TL (Charles Walker), 11TR, 11R (Charles Walker), 45R (Charles Walker), 47TR (Charles Walker), 49BR (Charles Walker), 70R (Charles Walker).

Credits

Photography
Neil Sutherland

Editor
Philip de Ste. Croix

Design and page make-up
Stonecastle Graphics Ltd.

Model
Adele Ladkin

Production
Ruth Arthur
Sally Connolly
Neil Randles
Karen Staff
Jonathan Tickner

Director of production
Gerald Hughes

Typesetting
SX Composing Ltd, Essex

Colour reproduction
Pixel Tech Prepress PTE Ltd, Singapore

Printed and bound by
Sing Cheong Printing, Hong Kong

THE AUTHOR

Joan Moore is a journalist and an author who has studied with the Faculty of Astrological Studies and who writes extensively on astrology, metaphysics and the occult. Joan has a particular interest in the esoteric nature of the cat and has written a thesis on its myth and legend throughout the ages. A Fellow of the Zoological Society of London, Joan is also an acknowledged authority worldwide on matters feline, has written books and many other shorter works on the subject, and regularly consults on video, TV, literary and other cat-related projects.

INTRODUCTION

Foretelling the future by means of divination has long held a compelling fascination for mankind. And it continues to do so. For the ancients, divination was a means of explaining the inexplicable, for unravelling life's mysteries – and for predicting the future. There have always been seers, wise men and women, able to interpret nature's ways and these, the shamans, prophets and astrologers, were held in high esteem by virtue of their inherent intuitive and interpretative powers. Over the ages, the Tarot and cartomancy have established themselves as two of the most popular methods by which Man could learn his fate . . .

For those interested in learning the art of prediction or who wish to extend their studies, *The Amazing Book of Tarot and Card Prediction* will prove invaluable in furthering their knowledge. The opening chapters discuss the origins of the Tarot and they are followed by sections which explain the divinatory and reversed meanings of the Major and Minor Arcanas. All are photographically illustrated showing the rich and colourful imagery of the Tarot de Marseille deck. Significant terms and arcane symbols are explained in the section entitled "Mystical Meanings" and a variety of the decks available today are also illustrated.

Valuable insight into how to achieve the appropriate mood for a reading and tips on the reading itself, are offered; while pictorial examples demonstrate how to lay out an assortment of spreads complete with step-by-step instructions – you'll be surprised at just how simple it can be!

Layouts featuring questions put by an Enquirer, with detailed interpretations and illustrations, show clearly how to complete a reading. Favourite classic spreads, as well as some that I have specially devised for this book, offer a lively glimpse into the arcane mysteries of the Tarot.

Prediction by cartomancy (the use of conventional playing cards) is explained in Part Two. Though not as bold and colourful as the Tarot, cartomancy nonetheless is equally fascinating and as divinationally effective. We look at its history and study the deck and its interpretations. Did you know that parallels may be drawn between the playing cards and Time itself?

The suits and their meanings exemplify the theory that a deck of playing cards represents a medieval court with its Kings, Queens, Knights, Jacks and, of course, the mischievous Joker! As with the Tarot, cartomancy's various combinations of court and numbered cards bring an added depth to a reading. All of this is explained in simple terms, as are also methods of selecting client cards and significators.

Classic and some specially devised spreads with hypothetical queries are represented, again with photographic illustrations. The cosmic symmetry of numbers is also explained, since numbers play an important role in cartomancy. Highlighting this aspect of the subject, the predictive system explained on page 121 may prove a fascinating diversion from the more formal spreads.

Designed throughout as an instructive aid, *The Amazing Book of Tarot and Card Prediction* is a unique textbook, beautifully illustrated and offering deep and meaningful insight into the mysteries of fortune-telling by cards. J.M.

Part One

The Tarot

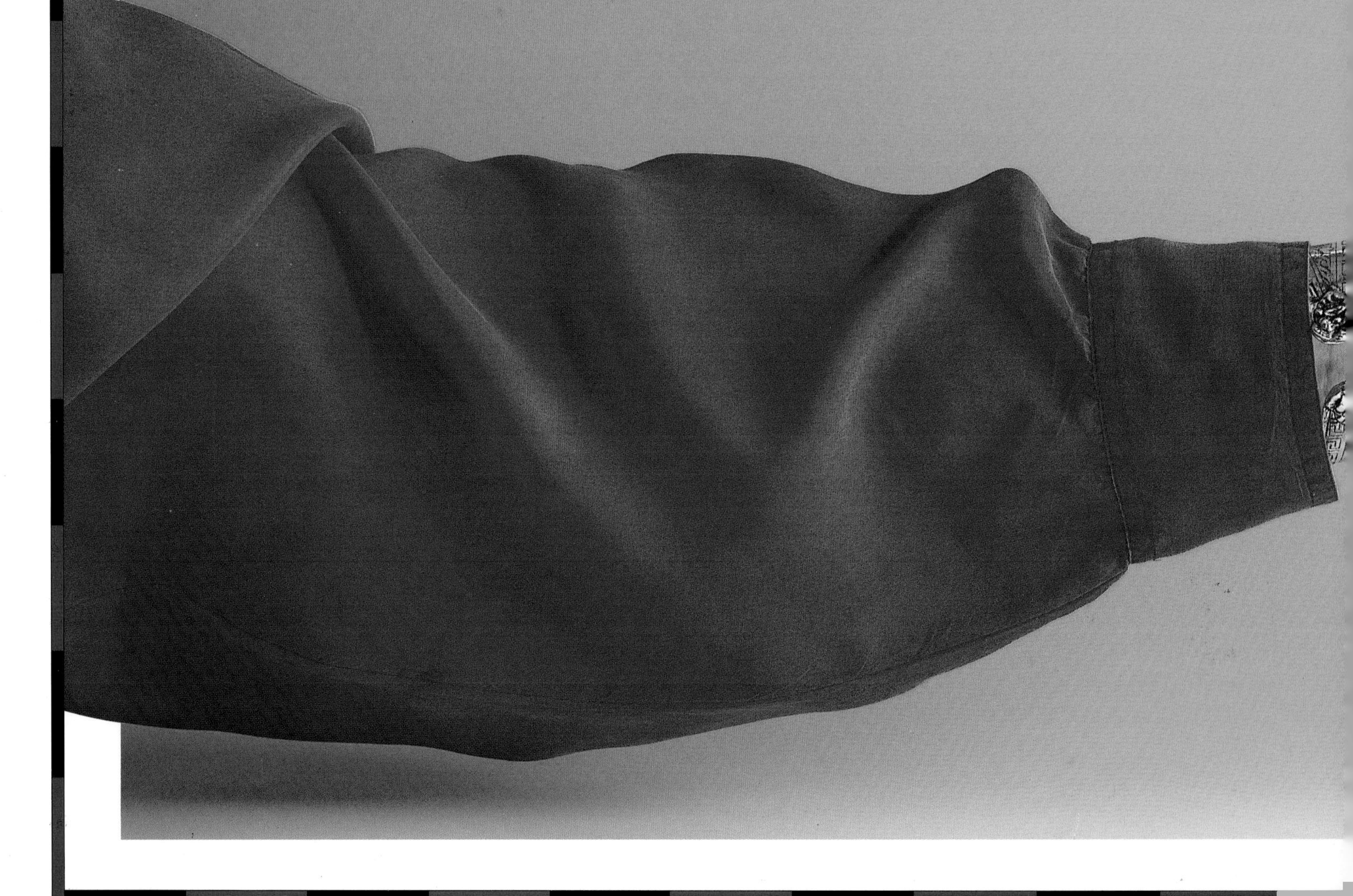

I
LE BATELEUR
THE MAGICIAN

THE ORIGIN AND HISTORY OF THE TAROT

A powerful tool of divination, the Tarot is said to embody the esoteric religions of Ancient Egypt, India, Chaldea (an area at the head of the Persian Gulf) and Persia, embracing also Hebrew Kabbalistic and early Christian beliefs. The images on the Tarot cards were mainly pagan in origin and the Dark Age dogma of the Christian Church referred to them as "the devil's books", linking them with black magic and witchcraft.

POSSIBLE ORIGINS

It is believed that the Tarot was first created in Alexandria, Egypt some 4,000 years ago. Another possible place of origin may have been Fez in Morocco, circa 1,200C.E., (Common Era [Jewish calendar], equivalent to A.D.), which would explain the presence of the Tarot mysteries in the Muslim world.

Tarot cards have been known to the West since 1392 when artist Jacquemin Gringonneur was said to have painted a set of cards for King Charles VI of France. Italian Tarot cards have enjoyed ongoing popularity since the mid-15th century when Italian artist Bonifacio Bembo created the Visconti Sforza deck in honour of the marriage between the Duke of Milan and Bianca Maria Visconti. In 1526, an Italian reference to the Tarot alludes to the game of "tarocco".

In the early 1780s French theologian Antoine Court de Gébelin who was fascinated by the lore of Ancient Egypt, maintained that the custom then had been to gather in the temple of Thoth, or Hermes. Thoth was the Egyptian god of science. The walls of the temple were hung with pictorial images depicting the major forces believed to influence life, and at these a loose bundle of rods would be hurled. The pattern in which they fell, in relation to the images, would then be interpreted by the priests. These proclamations were known as the "wisdom of the gods".

From this ritual came the practice of carrying around the unbound pages of the sacred Book of Thoth and subsequently any site could be used as a temple merely by producing the "pack" of cards. The Court de Gébelin pack of Tarot cards, designed around 1780, is believed to be the first "western" deck specifically used for divination.

Right: The Visconti Sforza deck designed by Bonifacio Bembo.

Below: The Moon card from the deck reputedly created for Charles VI by Jacquemin Gringonneur.

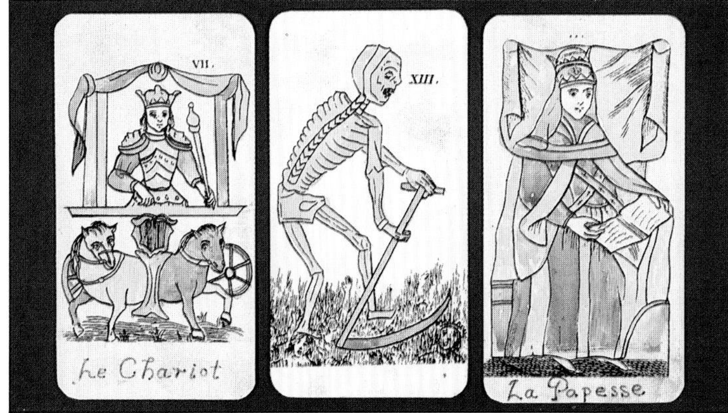

The Court de Gébelin deck (c1780) was probably the first "western" pack to be used for divination. Seen above are The Chariot, Death and La Papesse (The High Priestess) cards.

Left: Thoth, the ibis-headed Egyptian god of Science, as portrayed in *The Hymn to Osiris*.

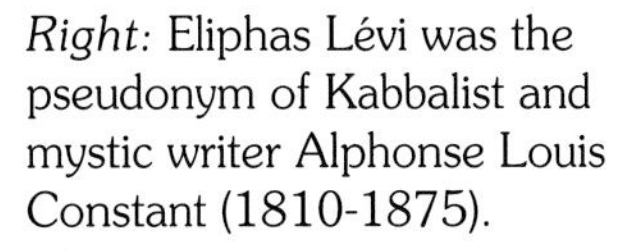

Right: Eliphas Lévi was the pseudonym of Kabbalist and mystic writer Alphonse Louis Constant (1810-1875).

Kabbalist Alphonse Louis Constant, more widely known as Eliphas Lévi, said in 1855: "The Tarot cards are the key to the esoteric tradition of the Jews" and, as a symbolic representation of The Tree of Life were the "primitive source of Divine and human Tradition".

A possible origin of the word "tarot" is the Kabbalistic "torah" which refers to the sacred texts of the Jewish religion. Another source could be the Latin word "rota" meaning "wheel", applying to the Tarot's Wheel of Fortune.

In 1889, French writer Gerard Encausse, using his pen-name Papus, enthused in his *Le Tarot des Bohémiens* that the Gypsies possessed a "Bible of Bibles", a card game called the Tarot which contained the basic wisdom of all ancient peoples. Papus, a member of the Kabbalistic Order of the Rose-Cross, was significant in forging a link between the Tarot, Rosicrucians and the Freemasons – a link developed by a group of people anxious to revive lost Hermetic and Gnostic wisdom. Initially an Hermetic Order dedicated to the esoteric arts of Thoth, Hermes or Mercury, the group, which included the poet W.B. Yeats, occultist Aleister Crowley, Paul Foster Case, Papus and others, formed The Order of the Golden Dawn in 1888. Changing its name to The Holy Order of the Golden Dawn in 1903, the Order finally broke up and ceased to exist by 1914.

In its deepest mystical meaning, the Tarot is the art or practice of assessing or divining the truths of "chance" and "meaning". The dealing and shuffling of the cards symbolizes the "chance" element and the interpretation of those cards, an attempt to discover the "meaning" of life and consequently, ourselves.

THE MAJOR ARCANA

Derived from the Latin word "arcanus", meaning "secret", the Major and Minor Arcana contain the esoteric wisdom of the ancients. The Major Arcana cards number twenty-two, equal to the letters in the Hebrew alphabet or, as it is sometimes known, the Alphabet of the Magi. These twenty-two cards are the key to the power of the Tarot and each is a potent force in itself.

SYMBOLS OF HIDDEN POWERS

The meanings of the twenty-two cards of the Major Arcana are both archetypal and divinatory, and symbolize forces which influence the lives of us all. The unnumbered card, The Fool, represents the seeker travelling along the path of life in search of knowledge and self-awareness, meeting a variety of challenges along the way.

The emblematic images of the Major Arcana, as generally seen today, became stabilized by 1748 in the Court de Gébelin deck. This is referred to as the Marseilles or Classic Tarot and is the one used to illustrate this book.

As with astrology, the Tarot offers a method of predicting events and personal character reading. In combinations (spreads) the cards are believed not only to foretell the future but also to affect it. However, the primary function of the Major Arcana is to stimulate the intuitive faculties of diviners who, by this method, can discover and interpret prophetic images from the vaults of their sub-conscious.

The Major Arcana (0-21) are as follows:

0:	The Fool	XI:	Force
I:	The Magician	XII:	The Hanged Man
II:	The High Priestess	XIII:	Death
III:	The Empress	XIIII:	Temperance
IIII:	The Emperor	XV:	The Devil
V:	The Pope	XVI:	The Tower of Destruction
VI:	The Lover	XVII:	The Star
VII:	The Chariot	XVIII:	The Moon
VIII:	Justice	XVIIII:	The Sun
VIIII:	The Hermit	XX:	Judgement
X:	The Wheel of Fortune	XXI:	The World

It could be said that the Major Arcana represents the cycle of creation and evolution – a picture of completeness and of the world.

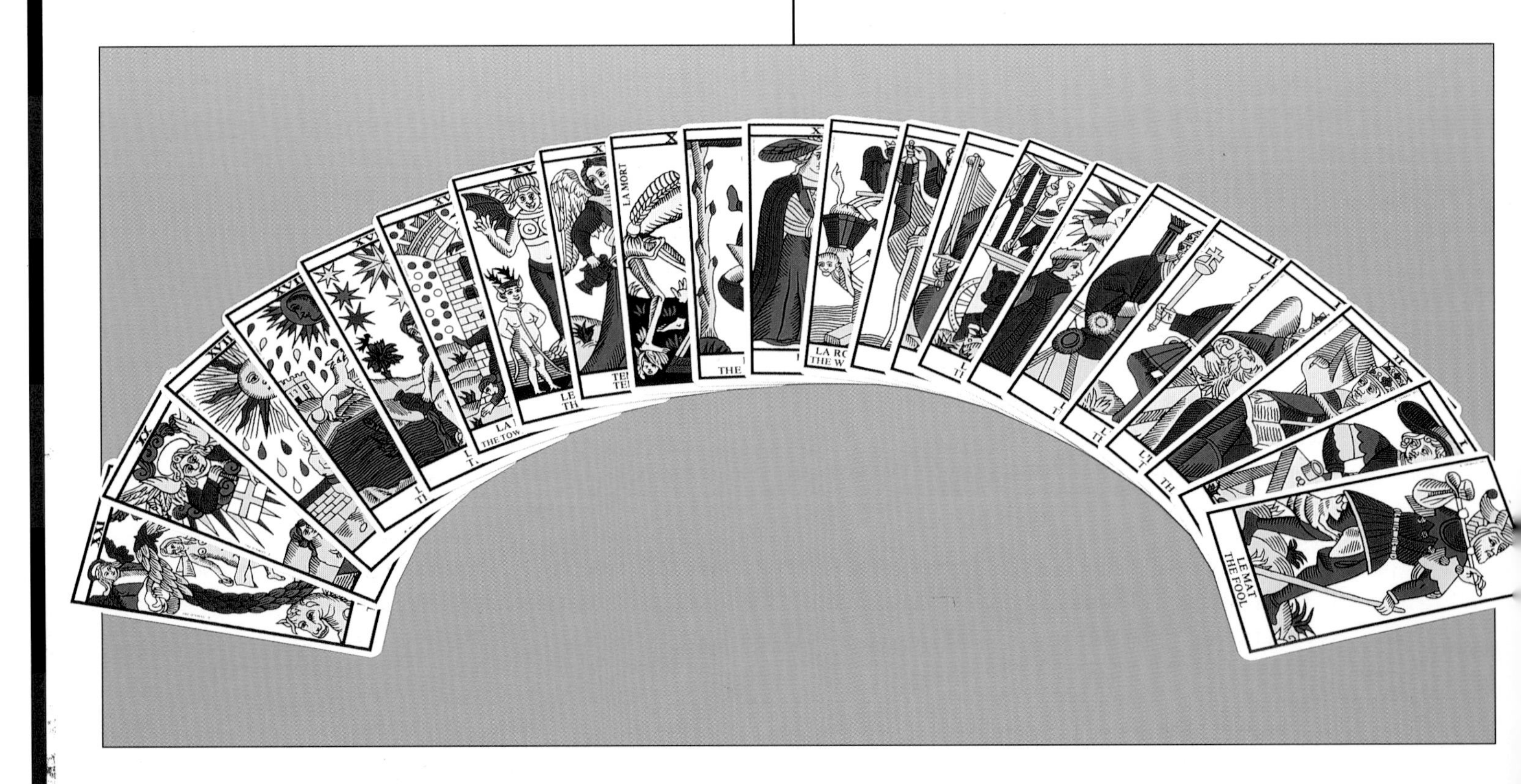

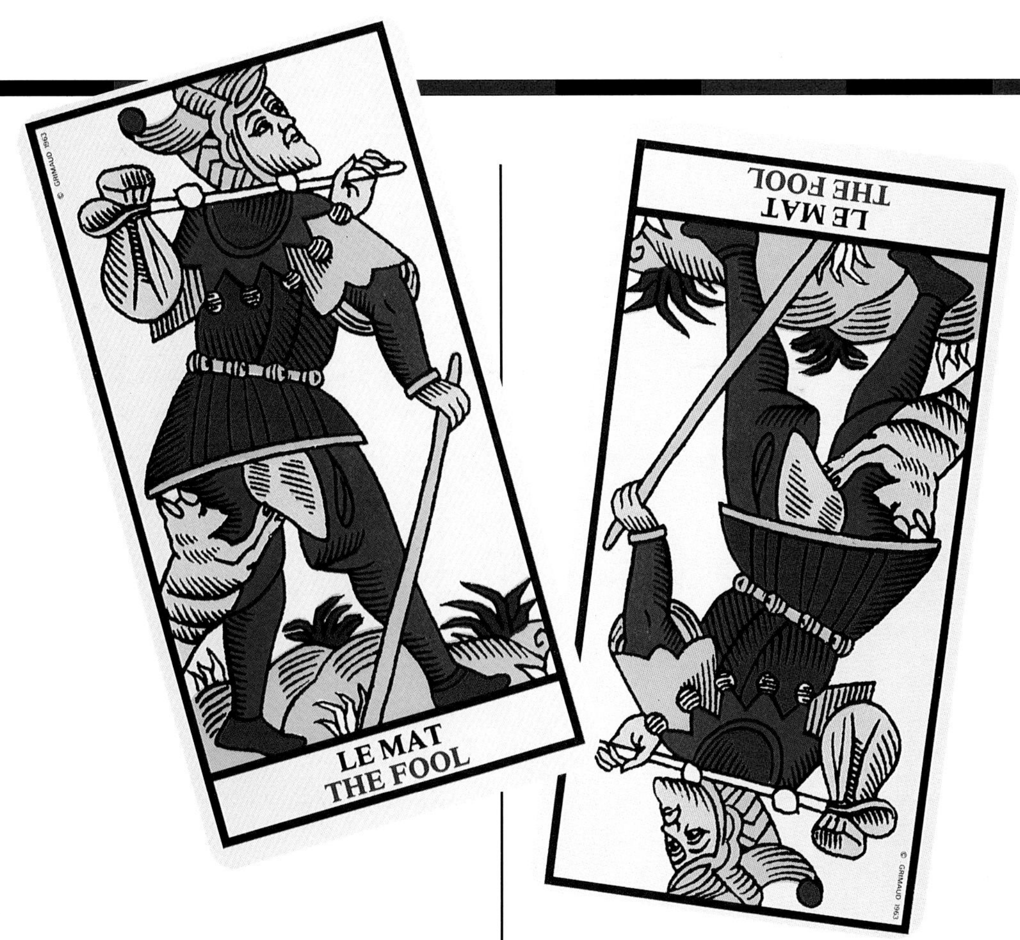

THE FOOL AND HIS JOURNEY

Edward Arthur Waite, an American scholar and mystic who wrote *The Pictorial Key to the Tarot* in 1910, describes the Fool as the "spirit in search of experiences". Like a child discovering life for the first time and, as yet, ignorant of the dangers and pitfalls which await him, the Fool is a young traveller embarking on life's path, inexperienced, impulsive, carefree, and careless. A seeker of Truth. The Fool carries few possessions – his pack is all he needs, implying few responsibilities or a lack of them.

Parallels may be drawn with Aries, the mythical being in astrology who marks the beginning of the Sun's journey through the Zodiac. This questing, self-assertive sign metaphorically sets out on its journey eagerly and fearlessly, meeting on its way the planetary forces which ultimately bring about its spiritual enlightenment and evolvement.

In the Tarot the number of the Fool is nought. 0 stands for Nothing. No Thing. Yet the circle of Wholeness stands for Everything. Such is the journey of the Fool. From Nothing he evolves and so completes the full circle, returning then to re-birth and new beginnings.

0 THE FOOL

With upturned face expressing energy and optimism, the brightly clad Fool steps out on the path of his supreme adventure. His pack holds but few belongings and his staff is held lightly in his hand. A small dog plays at his heels. Though likened to Aries (see left), the Fool card has no zodiacal or planetary ruler.

Divinatory meaning: The Fool is said to be the most potent, most volatile card in the deck. It contains all four elements and the danger lies in its potential for lighthearted folly and a willingness to take a leap into the unknown. There is a lack of discipline, a rashness and foolhardiness which needs to be controlled by effort of will. This card can also indicate a fresh start and new beginnings.

*When a card falls facing away from the Enquirer, or (as it would appear) upside down, this card is described as being in a "reverse" position. It can often hold a negative meaning in this disposition.

Reverse meaning: An ill-advised choice. Inability to make a balanced decision. Carelessness. Vanity and apathy.

I THE MAGICIAN

Suggesting hidden knowledge, the Magician averts his eyes and looks downward to Earth. His wand points upward to higher realms indicating that that which is above creates all things on Earth. Objects on the table await the Magician's touch to bring about change and transformation. To give the reader a clearer perception of the nature of each card in the Major Arcana, appropriate zodiacal, planetary and elemental forces have been variously used to describe each card throughout this section (see page 64 for celestial keyword interpretations). The Magician is the Aries card and its element is Fire.

Divinatory meaning: This card symbolizes creativity, originality and self-assertiveness with some arrogant pride. An ingenious individual. The first card encountered by the Fool on his journey, the Magician is initiatory; he creates new opportunities and gives the courage, driving power, skill and determination to bring these to fruition. Spontaneity. Movement. Self-reliance and control.

Reverse meaning: There can be weakness of will and purpose. Willpower may be used to evil ends and skills put to destructive use. Selfish, aggressive and quarrelsome behaviour. Deception. A cunning trickster.

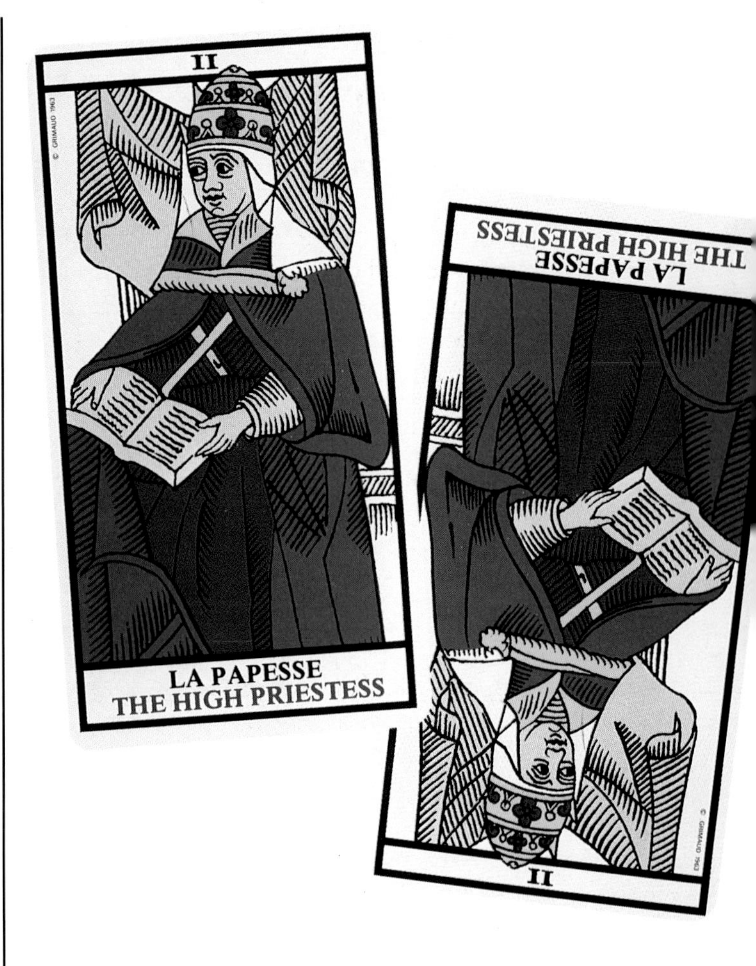

II THE HIGH PRIESTESS

A rich headdress adorns the head of the High Priestess implying a wealth of secret knowledge. A deeper wisdom awaits beyond the draped veil behind her head, for the Priestess is an initiate and is learning still. A book of ancient mysteries rests upon her knee, signifying that knowledge is revealed to those who are prepared to seek it out. This is the Pisces card and its element is Water.

Divinatory meaning: This card signifies the intuitive, inward-looking aspect of the self. The Fool sees the Priestess as his spiritual mother yet she symbolizes the virgin, the initiate with potential as yet unfulfilled. Representing the world of spirit. Natural insight. Enlightenment. Spiritual wisdom. This card also indicates studies of an occult nature.

Reverse meaning: Over-sensitivity to psychic influences. Ignorance. Physical vanity, emotional instability or outright deception. Selfishness. Superficiality.

III THE EMPRESS

This card represents the matriarchal figure. The Fool's earthly mother. Seated on her throne with serenity and confidence, the Empress is a woman of beauty and sensuousness, her fecundity reflected in her full-figured, possibly pregnant, condition. Her monarch's sceptre bears the inverted symbol of her ruling planet Venus and implies fulfilled womanhood. Her shield bears the golden eagle of wisdom. This is the Taurus card and its element is Earth.

Divinatory meaning: The Empress, goddess of creative arts and all fruition represents marriage, the fertility principle and motherhood. There is passion and sensuality in this card and also the ability to motivate others. Evolution and growth. Feminine progress. Achievement and accomplishment. Potential fulfilled. Happy, stable relationships. Material wealth.

Reverse meaning: Lack of self-discipline and over-indulgence in sensual pleasure. Inactivity and anxiety. A tendency to become domineering. Domestic problems. Barrenness.

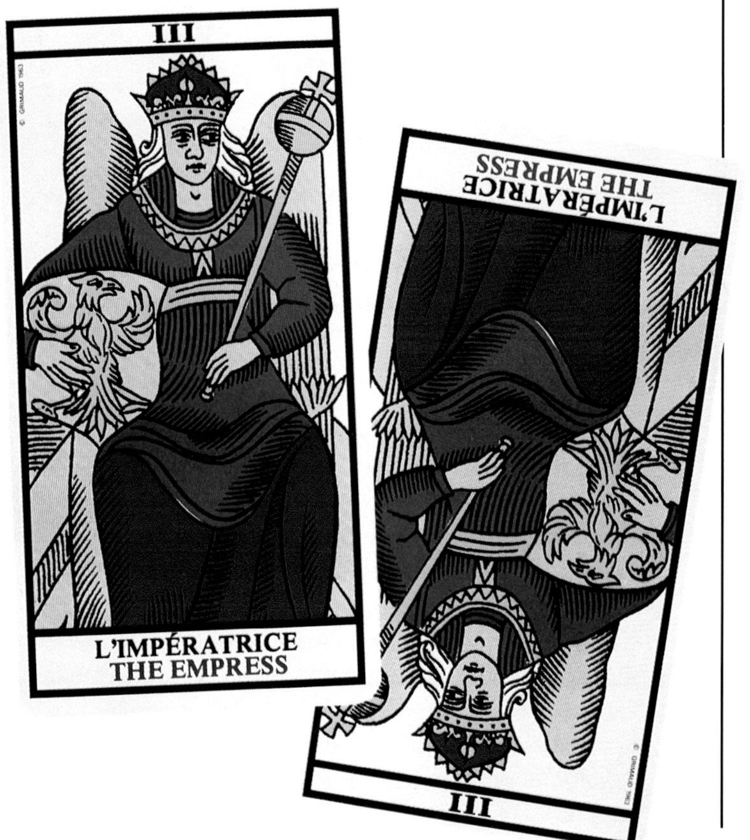

IIII THE EMPEROR

Confident and in relaxed pose, the Emperor, the Fool's earthly father, is the masculine counterpart of the Empress. Here is a man of majesty and strength; attributes tempered with patience and wisdom. His sceptre, a symbol of material wealth and status, is firmly grasped and he wears the golden chain of power and authority. The royal eagle is poised, perfectly balanced, suggesting discipline and self-control. This is the Capricorn card and its element is Earth.

Divinatory meaning: This card represents a dynamic force, powerful yet controlled, suggesting law, order, wisdom and rulership. The Emperor brings reason and logic to triumph over emotion and undisciplined ways. He also brings caution; practicality; perseverance; endurance and tenacity of purpose. Material wealth and stability is indicated.

Reverse meaning: A too-rigid discipline may lead to frugality and meanness. Stagnation. Foolishness. Feebleness. Ineffectual and immature actions with lack of emotional control.

V THE POPE

Symbolizing spiritual power, the Pope blesses those who kneel before him. Seated between twin pillars, suggesting earthly and spiritual spheres, he is the omnipotent mediator, offering kindly wisdom to all who seek it. Often seen in the role of Chiron, wise centaur of Greek mythology (and latterly included by some as a planet in the Zodiac), who taught mortal men spiritual values and the art of healing, the Pope embraces esoteric and conventional religions. This is the Chiron card and its elements are Air and Earth.

Divinatory meaning: This card signifies religions of all denominations and represents the Fool's spiritual father. It offers compassion, mercy, humility and a consciousness of higher realms. There is also an orthodoxy to the Pope, implying conventionality; marriage vows; a need for, or a love of, convention and outward signs of approval and conformity.

Reverse meaning: Foolish excess of kindness and generosity and an obsession with flamboyant ritual. Unconventionality and unorthodoxy. Gullibility. Rebellion.

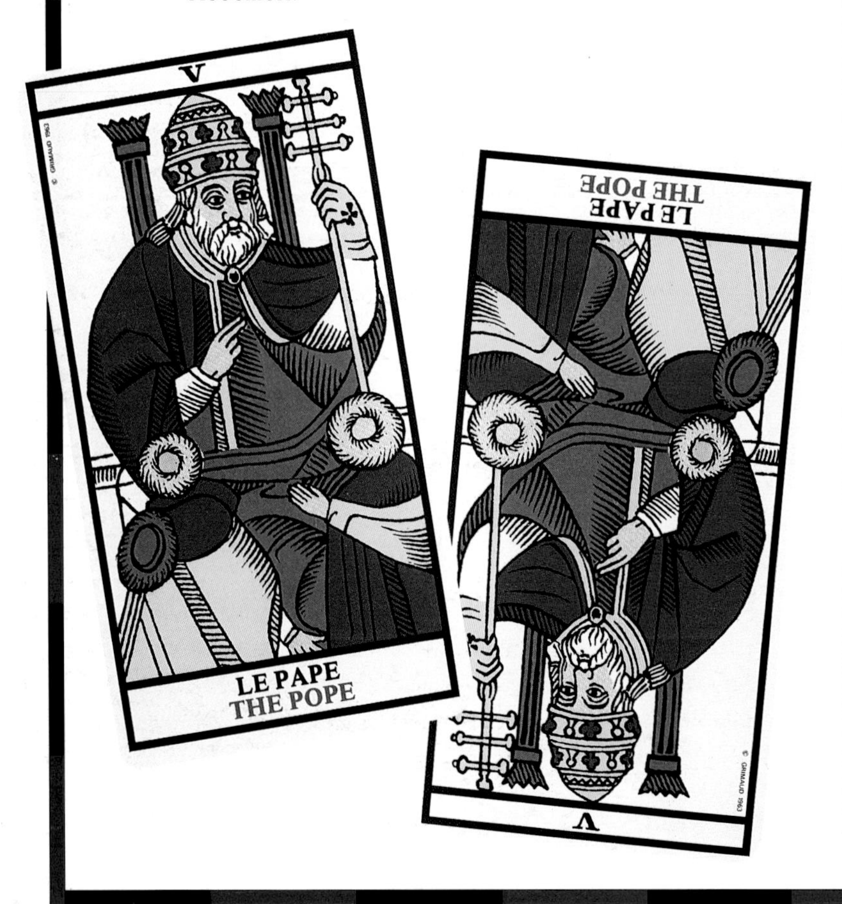

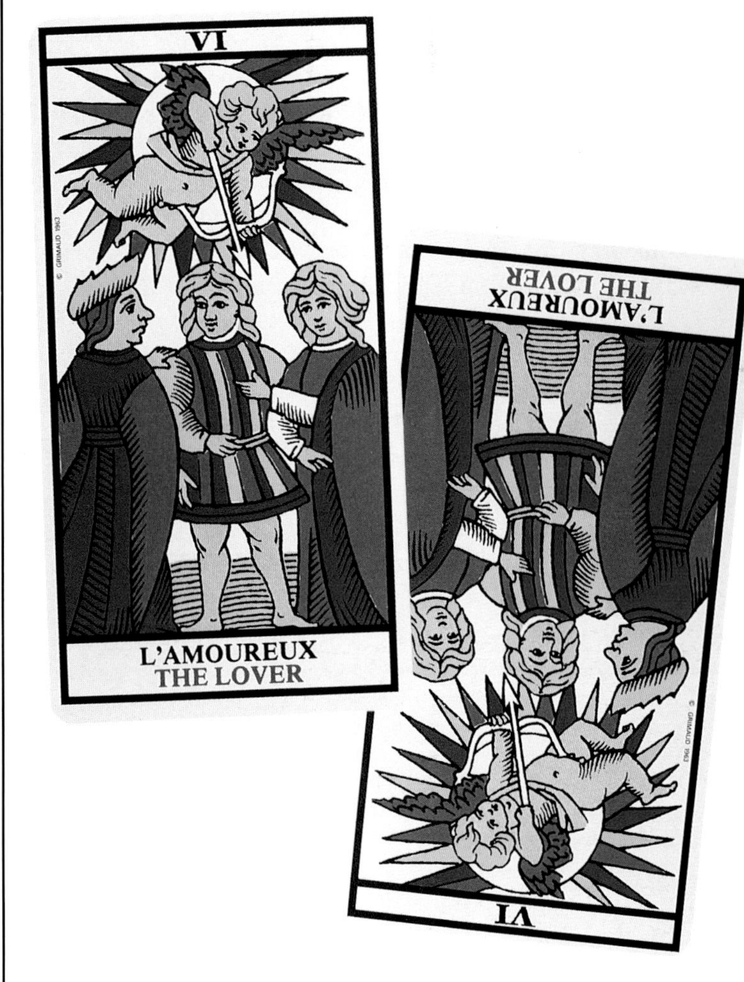

VI THE LOVER

A young man stands between a dark-haired woman and a golden-haired girl. Cupid, anxious to shoot his arrow of Love is poised above. The Lover, who could represent the Fool, must make his choice – the light or dark; the spiritual or the sensual. This is the Gemini card and its element is Air.

Divinatory meaning: This is the "choice" card. The Lover, under the influence of Cupid, is torn by indecision but, in order to make spiritual progress, he must make his choice. Card Six represents a time of speculation and putting to the test. Yearning. Temptation. The ability to make good choices. The possibility of a new romance. Change.

Reverse meaning: Infidelity. Family quarrels leading to separation. Dissolution of a marriage. Inability to resolve a personal problem or the possibility of making a wrong choice. Inconsistency. Unreliability.

VII THE CHARIOT

A crowned conqueror stands between four pillars representing the four elements. The epaulettes on his suit of armour suggest the opposing faces of conflict and his Chariot is drawn by two horses pulling in opposite directions. The Chariot wheels imply turbulence and unrest but the conqueror is triumphant: he has reconciled the diametrically opposed forces. This is the Sagittarius card and its element is Fire.

Divinatory meaning: Travelling life's path, the Fool now encounters inner conflict and discovers that true progress is made only when opposing forces are balanced and integrated. This card indicates that adverse powers can be conquered by willpower and self-control. Ascendancy over trouble. A middle course is steered. A balance of hard work (earthly) and periods of productive solitude (spiritual) are required. Travel or a journey accomplished.

Reverse meaning: Defeat. Failure to assert self-discipline. Collapse of plans. Loss of control. Vengeance.

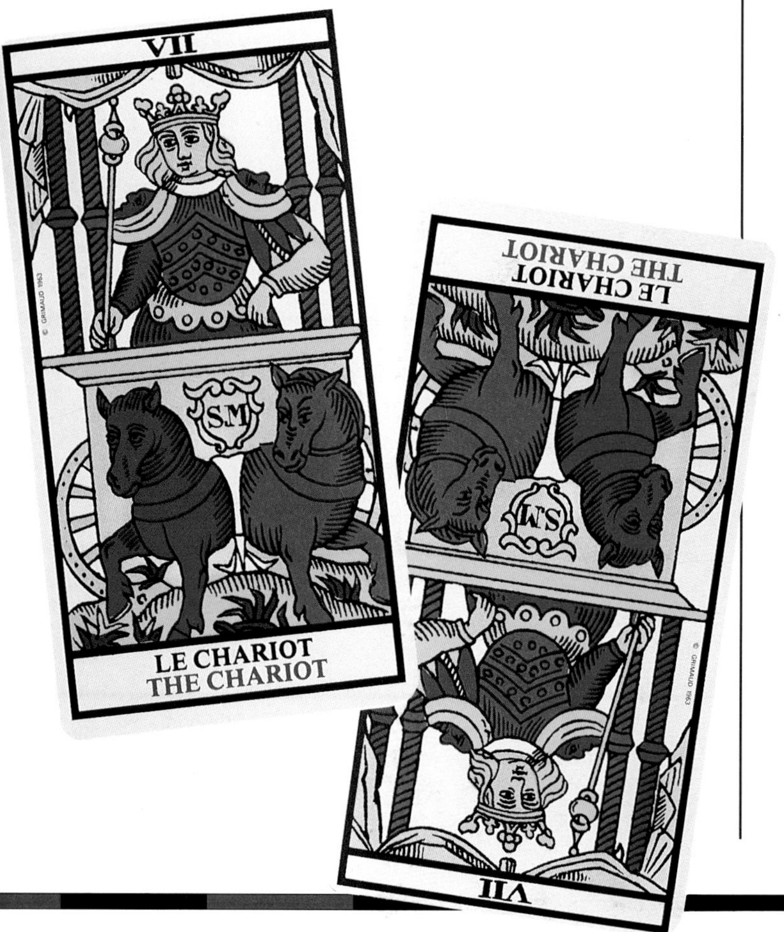

VIII JUSTICE

A crowned female figure holds the scales of Justice in her left hand. In her right hand the double-edged sword of the law is held resolute and firm. Twin pillars symbolize the eternal opposites or opposing forces in life. Justice is concerned with weighing up the balance, with integrity, fairness and reason. The Fool, on meeting card Seven, learnt that force can reconcile opposing elements. He now discovers that this may also be achieved by intellectual means, using logic and reason. This is the Libra card and its element is Air.

Divinatory meaning: Card Eight represents justice, making wise choices or decisions and adjusting to the situation following these. Reasonableness and fairness. Reason transcending emotion. Honour. Virtue. Legal matters are also indicated, such as lawsuits, divorces and wills.

Reverse meaning: Prejudice and bias. A lack of balanced judgement. Inequality. Bigotry. False testimony. Legal difficulties.

VIIII THE HERMIT

A bearded man in cowled cloak holds a glowing lantern high in his upraised hand. His staff of wisdom supports him on his way. An ageing man of great sagacity, the Hermit is the eternal seeker of truth and light. He journeys alone through a bleak and seemingly empty landscape. This is the Uranus card and its element is Air.

Divinatory meaning: This card symbolizes solitude and the need for withdrawal. The Fool on his journey discovers this need and that only by self-denial and quiet contemplation can inner peace be gained. Caution. Sacrifice and circumspection. Prudence and thriftiness. A journey. A search for spiritual goals. This card can also mean desertion and loneliness.

Reverse meaning: Imprudence. Hasty actions. Selfishness and a disregard for the needs of others. Immaturity. Childishness. Over-caution. Refusal to accept the world as it is.

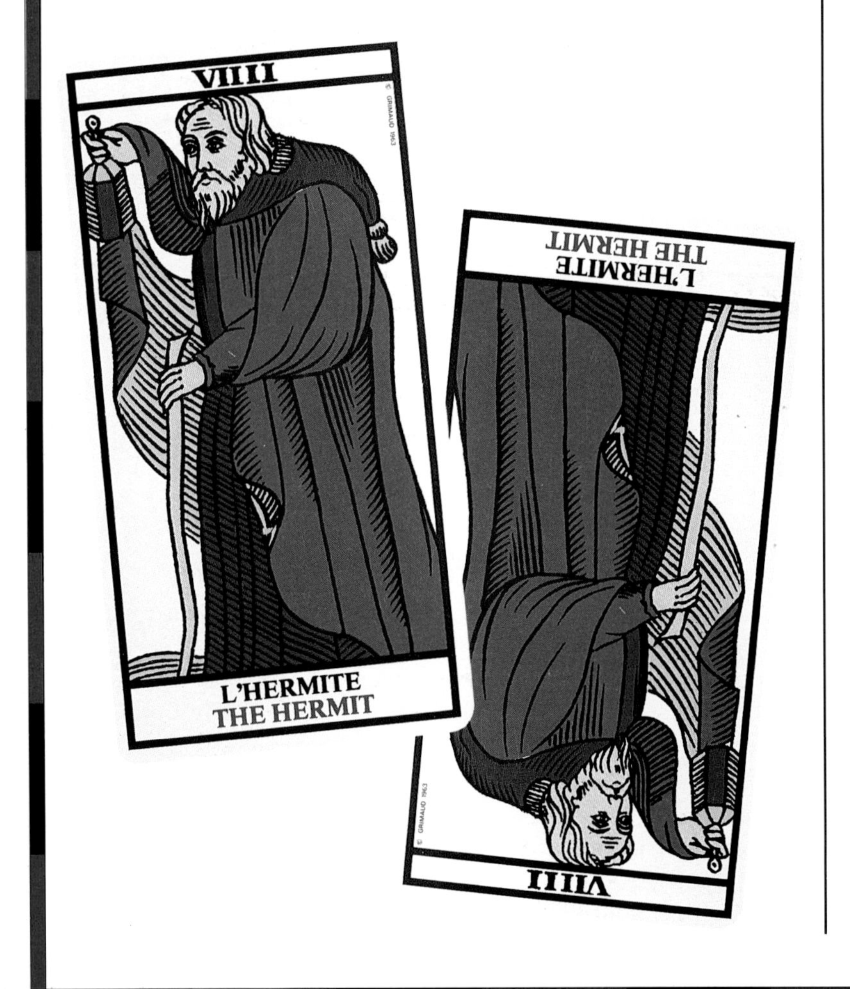

X THE WHEEL OF FORTUNE

A crowned figure clutching a sword sits triumphantly atop the Wheel. On the left-hand side another figure suffers a decline in his fortunes while on the right, another optimistically is carried upwards. There is a bizarre, incongruous quality to this scene, reflecting the incomprehensible game of "chance" dealt by the hand of Fate. This is the Mars card and its element is Fire.

Divinatory meaning: This card symbolizes cyclic evolution, indicating the compulsion and inevitability of its progress. The Fool learns that he alone must take responsibility for his life and not rail at Fate for his misfortunes. The Ten card suggests "time to move on to the next phase". Advancement for good or ill. The unexpected may occur. Good fortune.

Reverse meaning: Failure. Expected events take an unexpected turn. Ill luck. Good fortune eludes you. Inability to meet challenges.

XI FORCE

This card, also known as Strength, Courage, Fortitude or the Enchantress, symbolizes the ultimate feminine power – the Moon and fertility; mental and spiritual strengths. Calmly but firmly she is seen closing the mouth of the Lion who represents the Sun, reflecting masculine power and physical strength. Force signifies spiritual transcendency over the physical. This is the Venus card and its element is Earth.
Divinatory meaning: This card shows courage, strength and determination and with it is a self-awareness giving spiritual power. The Fool now learns the wisdom of self-discipline and the ability to control his physical lusts and passions. He has progressed one stage further along the path of personal evolution. Triumph over material power. Moral strength. Personal charm.
Reverse meaning: Abuse of power. An overbearing attitude – perhaps tyranny. Greed. Submitting to base desires. Weakness.

XII THE HANGED MAN

A man is suspended by his foot, not in the sense of death or torture, but from his own choice. He seeks new perspectives and in doing so sacrifices control of the conscious to confront unconscious forces within. His body represents two potent occult symbols – the cross, created by his legs, and an inverted trine of arms and head, which draws spiritual power from the unconscious world. Two trees bear twelve branches representing the twelve zodiacal signs. This is the Mercury card and its element is Air.
Divinatory meaning: Card Twelve indicates that sacrifice brings eventual rewards. Sudden insight. Rebirth. Transition. It is the conscious choice of the Fool to seek knowledge of the unconscious within. This card also indicates looking at a problem from a different angle.
Reverse meaning: Refusal to act or change oppressive conditions. Lack of effort to improve matters. Egocentricity and false spiritual claims.

XIII DEATH

The skeletal figure of Death wields a scythe, hewing down all before it. The ground is black and barren and severed limbs lie in disarray. Death, it is seen, is no respecter of persons and takes with it innocent child and crowned head alike. This is the Pluto card and its element is Water.

Divinatory meaning: The Death card indicates change, transition and rebirth and does not necessarily portend a physical death. It symbolizes personal transformation; the end of the old and the birth of the new. This could mean marriage, a new job or the beginning of a new era. The Fool discovers that the old order must die so that new life may begin and that it takes courage to meet new challenges.

Reverse meaning: Stagnation. Fear of change or new challenge. A metaphorical death with no subsequent rebirth. Inertia.

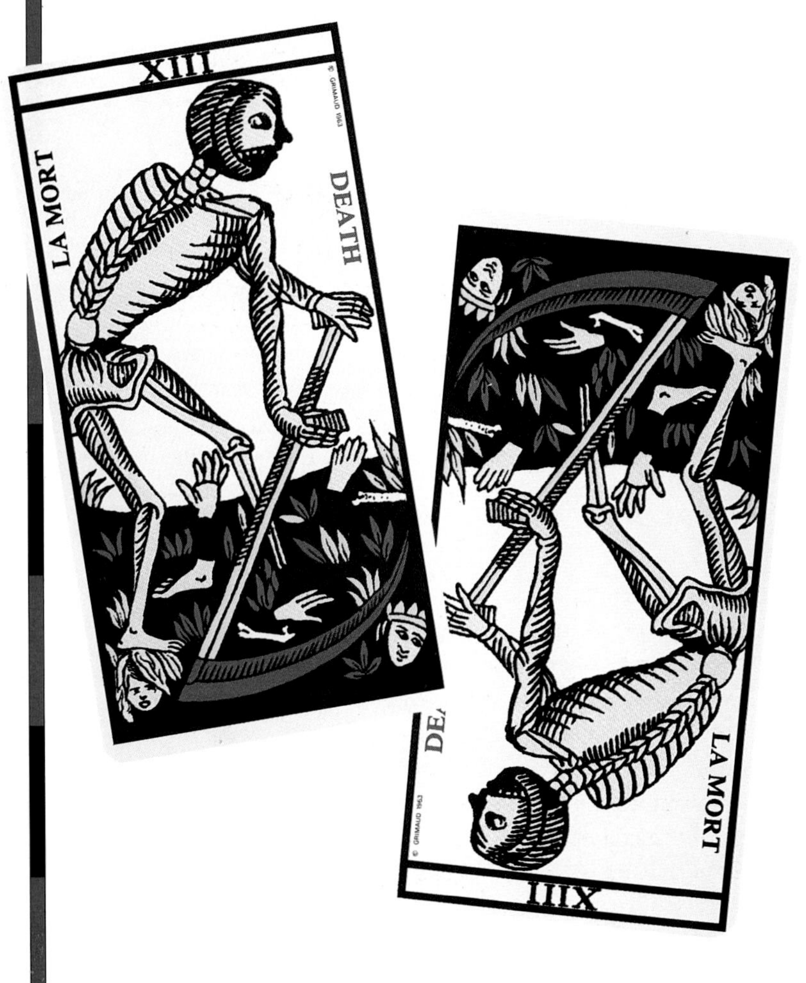

XIIII TEMPERANCE

One of the medieval cardinal virtues, Temperance symbolizes balance; time and its alchemy. The winged angel is poised and at ease, the waters of past and present flow between each vessel. None is spilt, suggesting economy and control. Transmuter of time, divine Temperance represents the harmonious integration of opposites: day and night; male and female; heaven and earth. This is the Jupiter card and its element is Water.

Divinatory meaning: The rhythm and harmony of Time past and present and the acceptance of its passage is the message of card Fourteen. It stands for successful union in personal and business relationships. To a balanced mind the Fool now brings the wisdom of a balanced heart; self-control and the capacity to modify and adapt when confronted by change.

Reverse meaning: Disharmony. Disunion. Discord. Inability to work with others. Unfulfilled desires.

XV THE DEVIL

The horned Devil stands with right hand upraised, signifying the black arts and destruction. His talons and short, dark wings suggest a dragon-like creature. A man and woman stand chained at his feet. From choice they have proved willing disciples and have already grown the horns and tail of their Master. Their remorseful expressions indicate that they now regret their allegiance. This is the Saturn card and its element is Earth.

Divinatory meaning: Forces for both good and evil are within us all. The Fool acknowledges and accepts the dark side of his psyche; this is not repressed but is channelled into a positive energy. It flows, unblocking negative urges and desires. The Devil card suggests enslavement or subservience to evil influences. Bondage. Self-punishment. Disaster.

Reverse meaning: Overcoming one's negative forces. Release from bondage. Spiritual enlightenment. Good comes out of evil.

XVI THE TOWER OF DESTRUCTION

A crown, symbol of earthly power, tumbles from the Tower as flames of fire descend from heaven. Also from heaven fall many yods*, Kabbalistic symbols of spiritual inspiration cascading to earth. Two men tumble headlong from the stricken Tower onto hilly ground from which already grow green shoots of recovery. This is the Neptune card and its element is Fire*.

Divinatory meaning: The old order breaks down so that the new may begin. To the Fool, the destroyed Tower signifies the shattering of his illusions, causing him to seek new philosophies upon which to re-build his life. This card represents order out of chaos. Learning through experience. New beginnings. Opportunity. It can also indicate unforeseen catastrophes; loss of security or the end of a relationship.

Reverse meaning: Imprisonment, physically or spiritually. Inability to abandon outmoded structures and bring about necessary change. Entrapment.

*See Mystical Meanings on pages 42-3.

XVII THE STAR

Symbolizing hope, renewal and inspiration, the Star is a welcome sight for the Fool, following his sojourn in the bleak underworld of his unconscious self. A girl kneels by a pool. She is Truth and her nakedness implies that she has nothing to fear; nothing to hide. She replenishes the pool with life-sustaining waters of conscious and unconscious aspirations. A bird alights on a tree and, as inspirational symbols of hope, eight stars gather above her head. This is the Aquarius card and its element is Air.

Divinatory meaning: The Star brings with it brilliant prospects; hope; new opportunities and success. Its magic may be fleeting but card Seventeen offers a beam of light where there is darkness. Optimism, insight and inspiration. The healing attributes of tranquillity and peace.

Reverse meaning: Pessimism; disappointment and unfulfilled hopes. Ill luck. A sense of futility.

XVIII THE MOON

Two dogs bay at the Moon while the yods falling to earth signify her powerful influence on those below. Towers standing either side symbolize the Moon's domination over conscious and unconscious forces. A crayfish crawls from a darkened pool, representing half-acknowledged and unknown fears. The Moon symbolizes intuition; inspiration; illusion and deception. This is the Cancer card and its element is Water.

Divinatory meaning: Card Eighteen represents the deep unconscious and distant memory, fantasy, dreams and emotions. The Fool, refreshed from his encounter with the Star, now discovers the feminine, negative, receptive and deep emotional aspects of his nature. This card implies falsehood; double dealing; false friends. It can also indicate illusion; escapism; self-deception; fluctuation and change.

Reverse meaning: Uncertainty. Unreasonable fears. Deception and trifling mistakes may occur. Control imagination in the interests of progress.

XVIIII THE SUN

Father figure; masculine principle; creator of all life; the bringer of daylight and hope, the bounteous Sun shines upon two young children; a boy and a girl. The children represent all that is bright and hopeful for the future and they are showered by the yods of fertility and inspiration. This is the Leo card and its element is Fire.

Divinatory meaning: The Fool rejoices in the warm light of the Sun. He acknowledges the creative, positive and masculine elements of his nature and is full of joyful optimism. Card Nineteen indicates achievement, fulfilment and success. Energy and inner strength. Pleasure in all things. A happy marriage and often material wealth or rewards through hard work.

Reverse meaning: Loneliness and failure. Greed and insensitivity. Plans do not come to fruition. Loss of power in career or personal relationships.

XX JUDGEMENT

The angel Gabriel blows his trumpet. It is Judgement Day. In supplicatory pose, three people rise from their coffins in answer to the trumpet's call. They are unclothed, their earthly garments cast aside in favour of the nakedness of spirituality and truth. Black graves indicate the dark realms of death from which they have emerged. This is the Scorpio card and its element is Water.

Divinatory meaning: The Judgement card represents rebirth, renewal and rejuvenation. This, the Fool's penultimate encounter on his journey, offers heavenly rewards. His spiritual development is almost complete. Card Twenty indicates the need to assess ourselves and to atone, if necessary. It is important too that we learn to forgive ourselves and others, in order to move forward. Regeneration and reward for past efforts.

Reverse meaning: Regret. Selfish choice. Failure to face facts. Indecision and loss of material wealth. Previous transgressions may rebound.

XXI THE WORLD

Card Twenty-one represents completion; fulfilment; balance and harmony. Neither male nor female, an hermaphrodite figure stands or perhaps dances within a perfectly intertwined, oval garland – a symbol of integration and completion. Placed at each corner of the card are figures representing the four elements: the Angel signifies Water; the Eagle, Air; the Bull, Earth; and the Lion, Fire.

Divinatory meaning: The World celebrates the perfect integration and completion of a Whole which, in the Book of the Alchemists, symbolizes the completion of the Great Work. The Fool has completed his journey and all his previous trials and experiences culminate in card Twenty-one. The World indicates a spiritual awakening; desires fulfilled. Triumph. The final goal reached. Joy and a new life. Twenty-one is a most fortunate card.

Reverse meaning: Lack of vision. Failure to complete what has been started. Imperfection.

KEYWORD MEANINGS TO THE MAJOR ARCANA

0	The Fool:	Folly. Inspiration.
I	The Magician:	Transformation. Mastery.
II	The High Priestess:	Enlightenment. Insight.
III	The Empress:	Feminine progress. Creativity.
IIII	The Emperor:	Worldly power. Will.
V	The Pope:	Religious or spiritual power. Inspiration.
VI	The Lover:	Temptation. Relationships. Harmony.
VII	The Chariot:	Triumph. Victory.
VIII	Justice:	Reason. Integrity.
VIIII	The Hermit:	Caution. Prudence.
X	The Wheel of Fortune:	Destiny. Change.
XI	Force:	Resolution. Fortitude.
XII	The Hanged Man:	Insight. Transition.
XIII	Death:	Death. Change.
XIIII	Temperance:	Moderation. Self-control.
XV	The Devil:	Enslavement. Subordination.
XVI	The Tower of Destruction:	Downfall. New beginnings.
XVII	The Star:	Hope. Optimism.
XVIII	The Moon:	Deception. Intuition.
XVIIII	The Sun:	Happiness. Success.
XX	Judgement:	Regeneration. Rejuvenation.
XXI	The World:	Completion. Fulfilment.

THE MINOR ARCANA

The Tarot pre-dates conventional playing cards and the fifty-six cards of the Minor Arcana are the antecedents of the modern day pack of cards. The Clubs (also called Wands or Staves), Cups, Swords and Coins (also called Pentacles or Deniers), the suits of the Tarot, correspond respectively with the Clubs, Hearts, Spades and Diamonds of conventional playing cards. The reason that the Minor Arcana has fifty-six cards instead of the fifty-two of a modern pack is that each suit has an extra court card, the functions of the Tarot's Knight and Knave (or Page) being combined in the Jack of a normal card suit.

SYMBOLISM OF THE SUITS

The four suits of the Minor Arcana represent the divisions of society: Clubs, the serfs or peasants; Cups, the Church; Swords, the military and nobility; Coins, the merchants. India is shown to have links with the Tarot as, in that country, the four suits of the Minor Arcana represent the four castes of Hinduism: Clubs, the serfs or Sudras; Cups, the priests or Brahmins; Swords, the warriors or Kshatriyas; and Coins, the merchants or Vaisyas.

Kabbalist Eliphas Lévi also connected the four suits of the Minor Arcana with the letters forming the unpronounceable and revered name of God: JHVH. J: Clubs and its corresponding element Fire; H: Cups and Water; V: Swords and Air; H: Coins and Earth. Lévi also maintained that the letters of the Hebrew alphabet corresponded to the 22 paths of the Kabbalistic Tree of Life which, among other things, illustrates how the world came into being through the Ten Divine Sephiroth (Intelligences), which is symbolized in the Minor Arcana cards one through to ten.

Many diviners find that the 22 cards of the Major Arcana are adequate for their requirements, but a study of the Minor Arcana is recommended to enrich the student's knowledge of the Tarot. The images on the cards of the Minor Arcana are much more simple than those of the Major Arcana, but the meanings of each, nonetheless, carry an equally strong and vibrant message.

When dealing with the Minor Arcana cards, specifically in the case of the *Tarot de Marseille* deck used in this book, a "reversed" card may generally be ascertained by the fact that © *GRIMAUD 1963* is seen to be at the bottom right-hand side of the card when it is reversed. Alternatively, a small pencil mark placed on the face of the card, at one end, can easily identify the orientation of a card and so determine when a card appears in "reverse" position.

CLUBS * FIRE * INTUITION

Clubs are ardent and keen and burn with enthusiasm in the manner of their element Fire. They are aspiring, intuitive and impulsive. Representing our will and positive energy drives, Clubs can flare with an all-consuming passion. Conversely, their "fire" can quickly fade and die without other elements to stabilize its exuberance. Clubs are assertive, creative and initiatory with flashes of intuitive inspiration giving birth to brilliant ideas.

KING OF CLUBS

Warm, humorous and generous. Noble in defence of principle. Poised for action.
Divinatory meaning: Fair-haired man, impulsive, clever; tends to make instant decisions. Family man or friend.
Reverse meaning: Exaggerated ideas. Severity. Opposition.

QUEEN OF CLUBS

A noble woman, dynamic, independent, fascinating.
Divinatory meaning: Fair-haired woman who is a formidable rival to other women. Success in business.
Reverse meaning: Jealousy. Treachery. Failure in business.

KNIGHT OF CLUBS

Creative, resourceful, energetic young man who seeks adventure.
Divinatory meaning: A journey. Change of home. Opportunity leading to change. Departure.
Reverse meaning: Discord. Broken relationships. Unexpected or unwanted change.

KNAVE OF CLUBS

Cheerful, impulsive, fair-haired child or young person bearing good news.
Divinatory meaning: Good news. Birth of a child. Stranger with good intentions. Bringer of enthusiastic optimism.
Reverse meaning: Ill intent. Bad news. Reluctance. Indecision.

CLUBS

TEN

Divinatory meaning: Heavy burdens. Responsibilities. Self-imposed mental or physical problems can be resolved by enquirer's own efforts.
Reverse meaning: Treachery. Subterfuge. Seemingly insurmountable difficulties.

NINE

Divinatory meaning: Through reserves of strength, courage and endurance, challenge and opposition may be overcome.
Reverse meaning: Adversity. Disaster. Obstacles.

EIGHT

Divinatory meaning: Travel. Activity. Hasty decisions. Speed. Sudden progress. Initiative and action to the fore.
Reverse meaning: Dispute. Discord. Quarrels.

SEVEN

Divinatory meaning: Strength and determination overcome great odds. Courage. Knowledge and teaching skills.
Reverse meaning: Uncertainty. Anxiety. Hesitancy leads to loss.

SIX

Divinatory meaning: Conquest. Achievement. Success. Acclamation. Just reward for commendable effort. Good news.
Reverse meaning: Fear. Apprehension. Indecision. Delay.

FIVE

Divinatory meaning: Struggle. Opposition. Minor difficulties in all areas of life. At odds with others.
Reverse meaning: Possible lawsuits. Frustration. Contradictions.

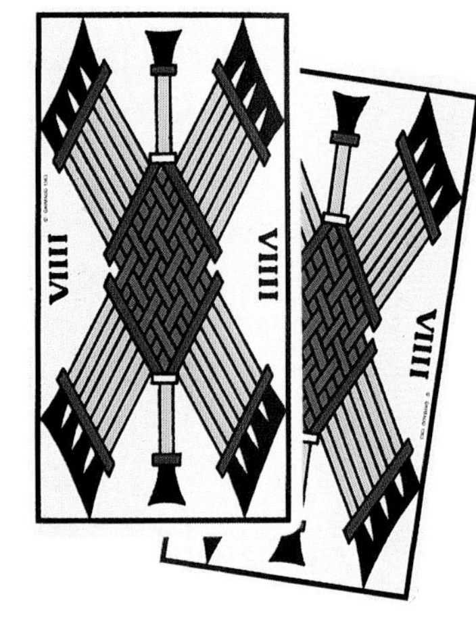

FOUR

Divinatory meaning: Happiness. Harmony. Peace. Romance. Rewards reaped. Prosperity.
Reverse meaning: Disharmony. Insecurity. Desires unfulfilled.

THREE

Divinatory meaning: Satisfaction. Goals achieved but there is more to accomplish. Negotiations. Business enterprise.
Reverse meaning: Offers of assistance may come with ulterior motives. Treachery. Loss.

TWO

Divinatory meaning: Partnerships with potential unfulfilled. Restlessness. Change. Strength overcomes obstacles.
Reverse meaning: Delay caused by others. Disillusionment. Melancholy.

ONE

Divinatory meaning: Energies renewed. Inspiration. Initiative. Ambition. Progress. New project or birth of a child.
Reverse meaning: Goals realized. False start. Decadence.

CLUBS: A SUMMARY

Intuition and inspiration will quickly flare and fade away, without the presence of other elements to balance their energy. Fire brings impulsive, impetuous action with some insensitivity to the feelings of others.

I Creation. New beginnings.
II Willpower can reconcile opposites.
III Growth, expansion. Eventual fruition.
IIII Labour followed by reward.
V Difficulties and opposition.
VI Conquering hero.
VII Wisdom and determination prevail.
VIII Movement and haste.
VIIII All elements combine for success.
X Problems resolved by personal effort.

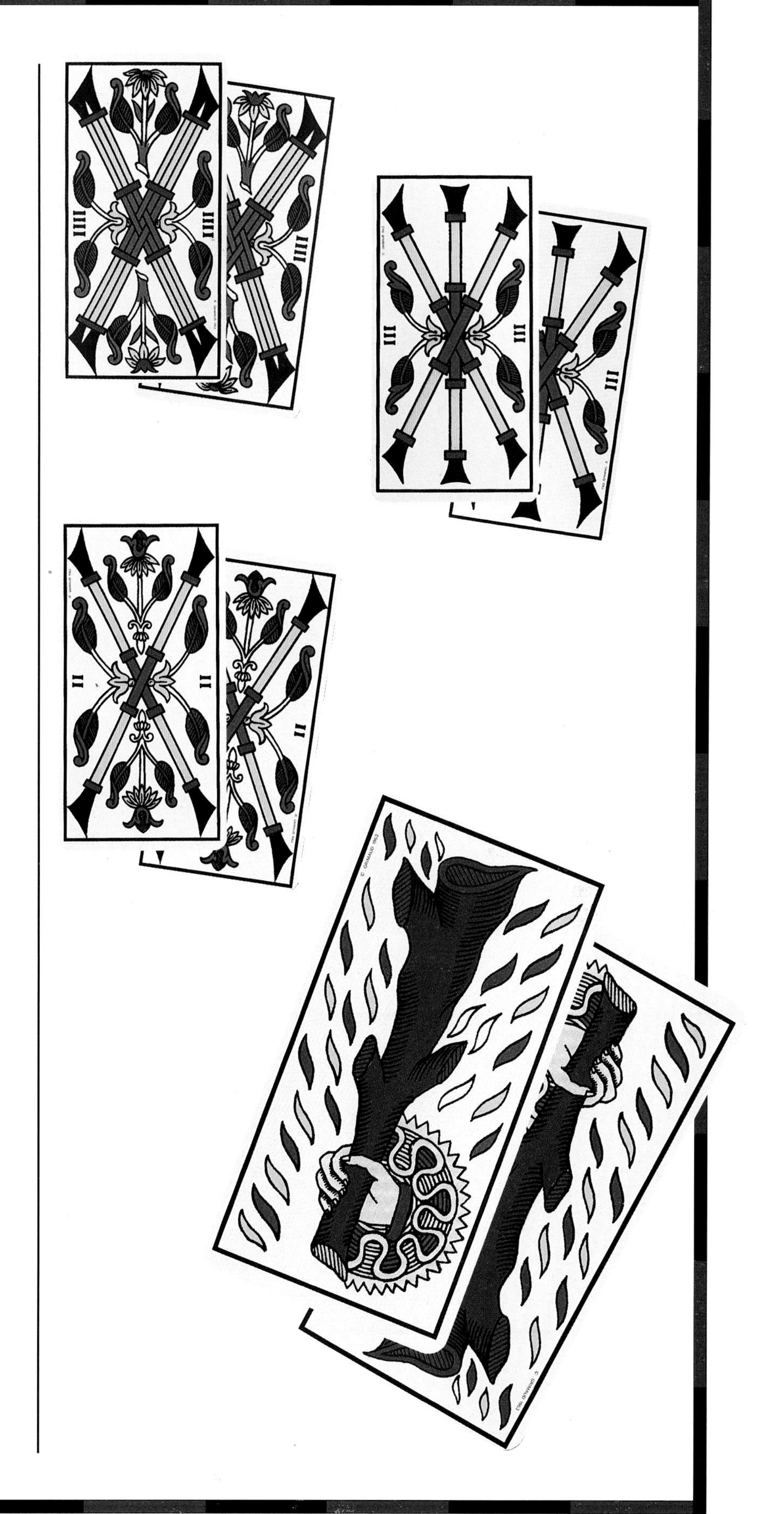

CUPS * WATER * FEELING

Cups represent emotions, inner feelings and are in touch with the psychic sphere of existence. Desires, intuitive instincts and far-distant memory spring from the fluidity of their constantly shifting element, Water. Cups are receptive, reflective, contemplative and often deceptive. Their compassion for others can overwhelm and their concerns lie predominantly in the realms of fantasy, imagination, romance, relationships and affairs of the heart. Cups can imply religious or artistic leanings.

KING OF CUPS

Generous, compassionate. Emotionally controlled and spiritually aware.
Divinatory meaning: Artistic or religious person with light brown hair. The requirement to relate to inner feelings.
Reverse meaning: Unreliability. Double dealing. Unpredictable temperament.

QUEEN OF CUPS

Affectionate woman; caring, sympathetic with intuition and vision.
Divinatory meaning: Charming, fair-haired woman. Good friend and mother. Devoted wife. Mystical and perhaps prophetic.
Reverse meaning: Immorality. Dishonesty. Emotional excesses. Untrustworthy woman.

KNIGHT OF CUPS

Romantic young man. Gentle; sincere. Contemplative; reflective.
Divinatory meaning: An invitation or opportunity may soon arise. Marriage proposal. Seduction. Judgement clouded by emotion.
Reverse meaning: Trickery. Fraud. Untrustworthy person.

KNAVE OF CUPS

Artistic child or young person. Reflective. Meditative.
Divinatory meaning: Birth of a new idea. New feelings and attitudes. Love of a young person or pet animal. Renewed trust.
Reverse meaning: Temporary distraction. Problems. Susceptibility.

CUPS

TEN

Divinatory meaning: Contentment. Happy family life. Love given and received. Joy.
Reverse meaning: Family quarrels. Strife. Disharmony. Loss of friendship.

NINE

Divinatory meaning: Pleasurable pursuits. Material wealth. Spiritual wellbeing.
Reverse meaning: Material loss. Emotional insecurity. Mistakes.

EIGHT

Divinatory meaning: Abandonment of previous plans. End of an era. Disappointment. Disillusion.
Reverse meaning: Completion of projects. Happiness. Material success.

SEVEN

Divinatory meaning: Choices made with care and consideration. Castles in the air. Fantasy. Daydreams. Very little achieved.
Reverse meaning: Will power. Determination. Desire.

SIX

Divinatory meaning: Memories of childhood. Nostalgia. Past influences. Reflection on personal talents.
Reverse meaning: Opportunities ahead. The future. Plans may not be realized.

FIVE

Divinatory meaning: Regret over loss, but something remains. New alternatives. Separation. Loneliness.
Reverse meaning: Favourable outlook. Hope. New friends.

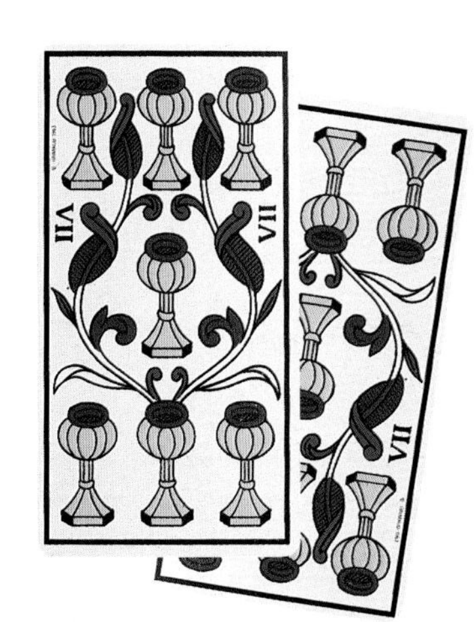

FOUR

Divinatory meaning: Discontent. Boredom. Spiritual confusion or unhappiness. Dissatisfaction.
Reverse meaning: New opportunities. New relationships or a fresh look at old ones.

THREE

Divinatory meaning: Fulfilment. Joyful event celebrated but more work lies ahead. Family matters.
Reverse meaning: Pleasurable excesses. Drunkenness. Emotional insecurity. Loss of happiness.

TWO

Divinatory meaning: Ideal balance of physical and spiritual love. Partnerships. Union. Harmony.
Reverse meaning: Separation. Disharmony. False friends.

ONE

Divinatory meaning: Spiritual renewal. New friendship. Fulfilment from love, marriage or motherhood. Fertility.
Reverse meaning: Emotional insecurity. Sterility. Barren relationships. Unfulfilled love.

CUPS: A SUMMARY

An excess of receptivity and feeling can indicate emotional vulnerability. Balance both spiritual and physical forces for completeness and wellbeing. Water is a powerful, all-pervading force and brings imagination and compassion.

I Joyful spiritual fulfilment.
II Balancing opposites.
III Achievement, but more work lies ahead.
IIII Discontent and confusion.
V Loss, but something may be gained.
VI Present and future opportunities.
VII Daydreams cloud decisions.
VIII Rejection of past plans.
VIIII Fulfilment of wishes.
X Perfection of family life.

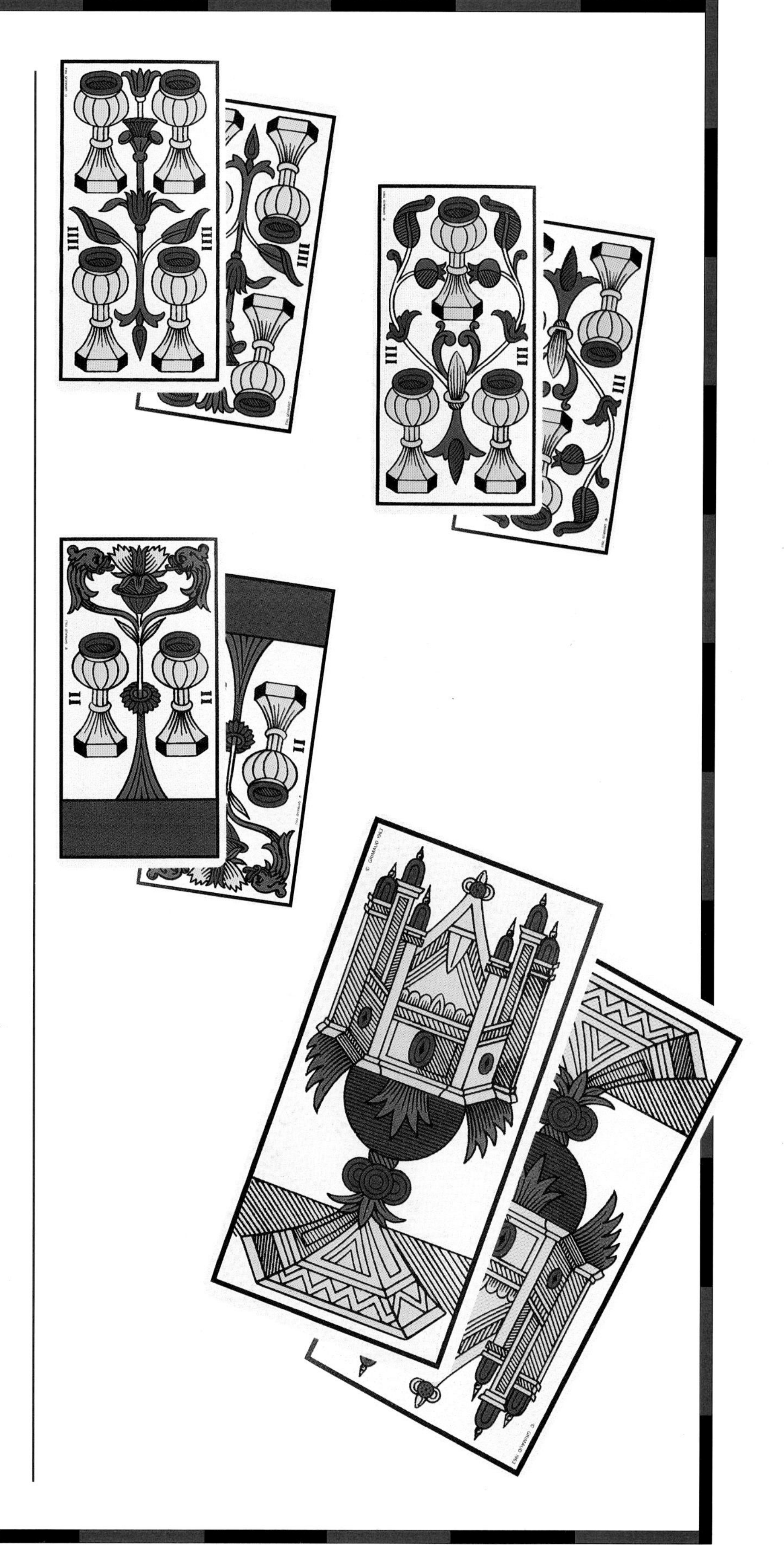

SWORDS * AIR * INTELLECT

Swords are intellectual and communicative and, like their element Air, are cool and free-ranging. They cut through muddled ideas and bring clear-cut reason to bear. Swords tend to lack emotion, rendering them insensitive to the feelings of others; in extreme cases, they can be bitter and cruel. Proficient communicators, conversation often has a "cutting edge". Swords work in the realm of ideas bringing into connection thoughts, people and places.

KING OF SWORDS

A figure of power and authority. Meticulous and scrupulous in his dealings.
Divinatory meaning: Brown-haired man with brown eyes. Controlled and highly analytical. Professional man. Law. Judgement.
Reverse meaning: Cruelty. Sadism. Dangerous person. Lawsuits.

QUEEN OF SWORDS

Intelligent, articulate woman. Shrewd and inventive. Widow or a woman who is withdrawn or sad.
Divinatory meaning: Privation. Widowhood. Beware of bitterness and withdrawal from others.
Reverse meaning: Vengefulness. Prejudice. Pettiness. Prudishness.

KNIGHT OF SWORDS

Aggressive young man, prepared to fight with skill and courage.
Divinatory meaning: Brilliant intellect. Good business acumen. Bravery. Headstrong rush into the unknown (see surrounding cards).
Reverse meaning: Impulsive mistakes. Impatience. Extravagance.

KNAVE OF SWORDS

Perceptive child or young person. An adept spy, indifferent to others.
Divinatory meaning: Disruptive situations due to gossip or rumour-mongering. Agility.
Reverse meaning: Bad news. Untrustworthiness. Unforeseen events. An impostor.

SWORDS

TEN

Divinatory meaning: End of a relationship or phase. Loss. Desolation. Ground cleared for something new.
Reverse meaning: Temporary gain. Profit. New ideas.

NINE

Divinatory meaning: Fear of disaster is greater than the outcome. Mental anguish. Anxiety. Concern for a loved one.
Reverse meaning: Doubt. Suspicion. Conflict with partner.

EIGHT

Divinatory meaning: Bound by personal fears. Inability to escape problems. Blindness. Confusion. Indecision.
Reverse meaning: Treachery in the past. Regeneration. Victory over fears.

SEVEN

Divinatory meaning: Objective gained by evasion and quick thinking. Logic and reason win the day.
Reverse meaning: Flight from unlawful act. Uncertain counsel. Unwise advice.

SIX

Divinatory meaning: A journey, perhaps across water. Tension and strain followed by harmonious conditions.
Reverse meaning: No solutions to troubles. No progress. Stalemate.

FIVE

Divinatory meaning: Destruction. Turmoil. Defeat. Dishonour. Limitations acknowledged.
Reverse meaning: Uncertainty. Misfortune befalling someone close. Weakness.

FOUR

Divinatory meaning: Relief from anxiety. Respite. Recuperation. Solitude. Rebirth of ideas.
Reverse meaning: Activity. Thrift. Economy. Regaining that which is lost.

THREE

Divinatory meaning: Quarrels. Separations. Absence. Faithlessness. Broken promises.
Reverse meaning: Confusion. Change of mind causes arguments. Partnerships dissolved.

TWO

Divinatory meaning: Stalemate. Balance. Compromise. Truce. Impasse.
Reverse meaning: Treachery. Falsehood. Dishonour. Disharmony.

ONE

Divinatory meaning: Strength in adversity. A force for good against evil. New vigour to mental powers. New ideas. Progressive thought.
Reverse meaning: Disaster. Self-destruction. Strife. Difficulties.

SWORDS: A SUMMARY

Cutting through deception and illusion can be a painful experience, but truth triumphs over confusion. Air is cool and clear; it represents communications and the logic and reason of the intellect.

I Progress and promise.
II Courage to make decisions.
III Rifts in partnerships.
IIII Productive solitude.
V Knowing when to admit defeat.
VI Difficulties give way to peaceful times.
VII Intellect triumphs over aggression.
VIII Mental confusion.
VIIII Time to clear the mind.
X Metaphorical death and subsequent rebirth.

COINS * EARTH * SENSATION

Coins represent our physical being; reality; material things; our practical work and finances. Coins are steadfast, reliable, cautious and can lack imagination. Reflecting their element Earth, Coins enjoy earthy, sensual pursuits and the luxuries of life, generally acquired through the fruits of their labours. Coins can be suspicious of new ideas and insensitive to the feelings of others. They are practical in matters of finance and are particularly possession-conscious.

KING OF COINS

Prosperous and highly successful in a worldly sense. Noble, magnanimous and mindful of material matters. Cautious, reliable and somewhat unadventurous.
Divinatory meaning: Experienced leader. Mathematical ability. Material success. Fruits of labour gladly shared.
Reverse meaning: Corruption. Avarice. Grossness.

QUEEN OF COINS

Astute, dark-haired business woman. Practical, capable. Friendly and generous to others. Enjoys sensual pursuits.
Divinatory meaning: Wealth. Wellbeing. Generosity. Luxury. Security.
Reverse meaning: False prosperity. Mistrust of those close. Fear of failure.

KNIGHT OF COINS

Pragmatic, sensible and dependable young man.
Divinatory meaning: Reliability. Patience. Persistence leading to reward.
Reverse meaning: Inertia. Stagnation. Carelessness.

KNAVE OF COINS

A practical child or young person. Careful and diligent.
Divinatory meaning: Application to studies. Scholarship. A desire for learning. Pride in achievement. May bring a message.
Reverse meaning: Rebelliousness. Dissipation of energies and ideas. Illogical notions.

COINS

TEN

Divinatory meaning: Material security. Financial stability. Achievement. Family tradition and values.
Reverse meaning: Loss of family wealth or reputation. Poor risk.

NINE

Divinatory meaning: Physical wellbeing, comfort and status. Success leading to jealousy of others.
Reverse meaning: Self-satisfaction. Threat to possessions or person.

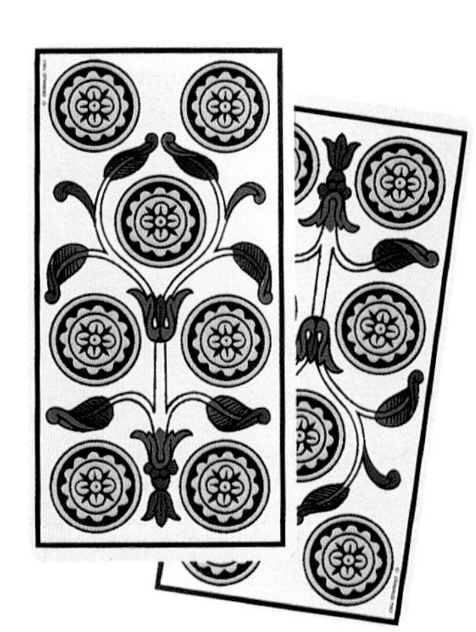

EIGHT

Divinatory meaning: Skills improved by practice. Craftsmanship. Apprenticeship leading to profitable career.
Reverse meaning: Lack of ambition. Failure. Excessive materialism.

SEVEN

Divinatory meaning: Success of past labours still needs consistent effort. Successful career negotiations.
Reverse meaning: Anxiety. Imprudent actions. Impatience over money.

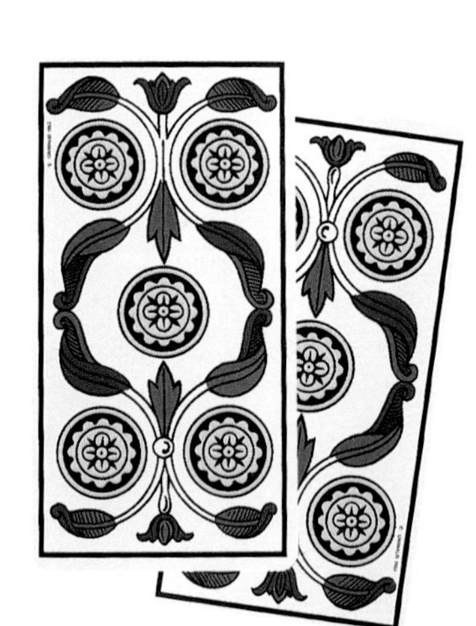

SIX

Divinatory meaning: Money matters on a stable footing. Loans repaid. Rewards from success shared with others.
Reverse meaning: Selfishness. Avarice. Envy.

FIVE

Divinatory meaning: Anxiety over money. Pay attention to detail to avoid material or spiritual loss. Impoverishment.
Reverse meaning: Reversal of fortunes. Confidence in the future.

FOUR

Divinatory meaning: Obsession with material wealth. Greed. Miserliness. Tendency to hoard.
Reverse meaning: Material and spiritual loss. Obstacles to further gain. Opposition.

THREE

Divinatory meaning: Foundations laid – finer details to follow. Achievement. Artistic ability.
Reverse meaning: Inattention to detail. Lack of skill. Money lost due to poor business practice.

TWO

Divinatory meaning: Dexterity in business matters. Agility. Fluctuating fortunes. New problems.
Reverse meaning: Indifferent business skills. Written notes. Accounts. Enforced optimism.

ONE

Divinatory meaning: Good beginnings for business. Substantial profit or gift. Status. Success. Security.
Reverse meaning: Obsession with wealth. Unhappiness. Corruption.

COINS: A SUMMARY

Coins represent all that is stable and secure in a material sense. But this aspect alone can mean hardness and corruption. Earth is the fertile base from which all things grow. It brings forth new life and is solid and dependable.

I	Labours rewarded.
II	Dexterity. Skill.
III	Success through effort.
IIII	Avarice.
V	Anxiety. Impoverishment.
VI	Stability.
VII	Consistent endeavour.
VIII	Profitable skills.
VIIII	Material benefits.
X	Home. Family.

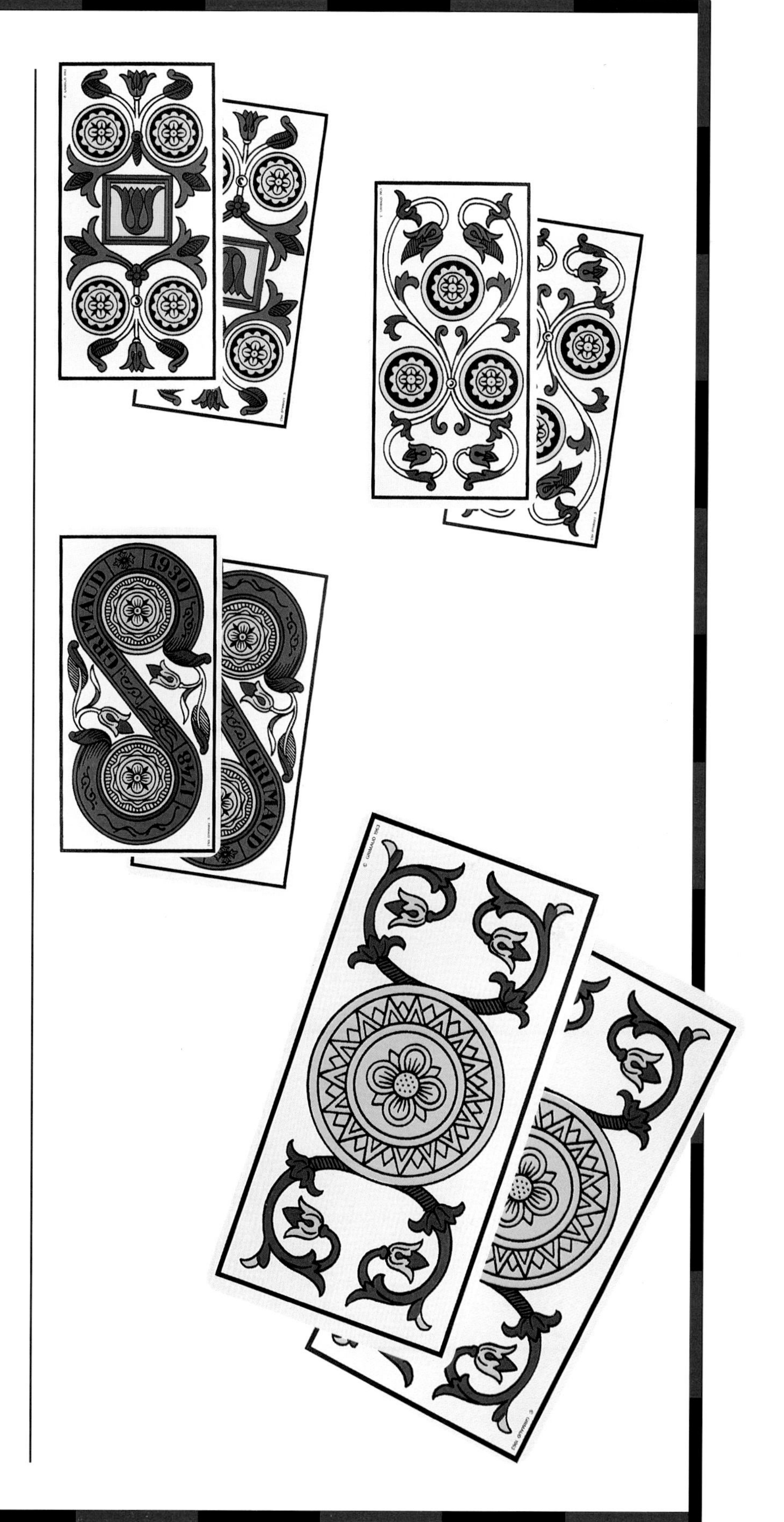

MYSTICAL MEANINGS

To summarize the preceding pages which describe the Major and Minor Arcanas, further explanations and key-word meanings are given below.

THE MAJOR ARCANA

It is said that the Major Arcana may be divided into three sets of seven cards: I-VII dealing with the conscious self, VIII-XIIII symbolizing change and the influence of others, and XV-XXI, the spirit, leading to the consummation of the subconscious self.

It has also been said that the first nine numbered cards represent the Enquirer's encounters with others and the last eleven depict the Enquirer's discovery of inner self. Between the two categories lies The Wheel of Fortune.

Cards I-XXI and their astrological correspondences

I	The Magician	Aries	Fire
II	The High Priestess	Pisces	Water
III	The Empress	Taurus	Earth
IIII	The Emperor	Capricorn	Earth
V	The Pope	Chiron	Air and Earth
VI	The Lover	Gemini	Air
VII	The Chariot	Sagittarius	Fire
VIII	Justice	Libra	Air
VIIII	The Hermit	Uranus	Air
X	The Wheel of Fortune	Mars	Fire
XI	Force	Venus	Earth
XII	The Hanged Man	Mercury	Air
XIII	Death	Pluto	Water
XIIII	Temperance	Jupiter	Water
XV	The Devil	Saturn	Earth
XVI	The Tower of Destruction	Neptune	Fire*
XVII	The Star	Aquarius	Air
XVIII	The Moon	Cancer	Water
XVIIII	The Sun	Leo	Fire
XX	Judgement	Scorpio	Water
XXI	The World combines the four elements of Fire, Earth, Air and Water		

* The combination of Neptune and Fire, not generally accepted as compatible forces, represents most effectively the powerful catastrophic elements contained in card XVI.

Yods Falling drops of light. Kabbalistic in origin, they represent the descent of the spiritual from heaven to earth. In the Tarot of Marseilles deck, yods appear in the Major Arcana on The Tower of Destruction (card XVI) and on The Moon (card XVIII). In the Minor Arcana, yods may be seen on the Ace of Clubs and the Ace of Swords.

THE MINOR ARCANA

Elements and characters of the suits

Clubs	Fire	Intuition
Cups	Water	Feeling
Swords	Air	Intellect
Coins	Earth	Sensation

Designated court card groups

King	Man
Queen	Woman
Knight	Young man
Knave	Child or young girl

Physical characteristics of the suits

Clubs	Fair hair and blue eyes
Cups	Light brown hair and pale eyes
Swords	Brown hair and brown eyes
Coins	Black hair and dark eyes

Court card keywords

King	Authority
Queen	Stability
Knight	Assertiveness
Knave	Receptiveness

In a spread, Kings and Queens generally represent actual people or aspects of the Enquirer. In addition to designated people, Knights and Knaves can often indicate events.

Keyword meanings of numbers I-X

I	Creation. Beginnings.
II	Opposites. Balance. Conflict.
III	Growth. Expansion. Fruition. First stages of completion.
IIII	Stability. Logic. Reason.
V	Uncertainty. Disruption.
VI	Harmony. Balance.
VII	Completion of cycle. Success. Progression.
VIII	Balance of opposing forces. Harmony.
VIIII	Power of the suit's element.
X	Perfection through completion. Consummation. End of the journey.

Cards with special meanings

Clubs

X	If near a good card, contradictions and obstacles.
VIIII	Bad omen.
VII	A fair child. A child for fair parents.
IIII	Unexpected good fortune.
III	A fortunate card. Collaboration and co-operation will further your plans.

Cups

VII	Light brown-haired child. A child for light brown-haired parents.
V	Good luck in love or with money.
II	Sensual pleasure. Success in business.

Swords

X	Next to an Ace or a King, imprisonment for a man; treacherous friends for a woman.
VIIII	Bad omen.
V	An attack on the Enquirer.
IIII	Beware.
III	Flight of a woman's lover.

Coins

X	House. Home.
VIIII	A "Yes", in relation to what is forecast by other cards.

CHOOSING YOUR TAROT CARDS

It is essential that you feel completely at ease with your chosen deck of Tarot cards and it may take some time before you finally discover your "special" pack. Tarot decks offering a wide range of themes and images are available at most esoteric shops and stores and often samples of the various decks may be examined before choices are made. Never choose your deck hurriedly, or when you are feeling insufficiently "centred" to make the right choice. Spend time to contemplate the ones which hold instant appeal for you. Those that "sing out" are in tune with your inner self and will ultimately enable you to give vibrant intuitive readings.

TAROT DECKS AVAILABLE

The Rider Waite Tarot (**1**) was devised by A.E. Waite for The Order of the Golden Dawn and designed, under his direction, by Pamela Coleman Smith. Issued in 1911, this deck is published by Rider.

The Classical Tarot features the standard Major Arcana images, while those for the Minor Arcana give the appropriate number of basic symbols without the complexity of additional pictures. Decks following this format are the Swiss 1JJ Tarot (**2**), the Italian Madonni Tarot, the Egyptian Tarot, the Spanish Tarot and the Tarot of Marseilles which has been used to illustrate this book. Oswald Wirth's Golden Dawn Tarot also features less complicated Minor Arcana cards, as does the stylish Art Nouveau Tarot by Matt Myers. The pagan path is followed by Richard Gardner in his Tarot of the Witches.

The strongly perceptive designs of Pamela Coleman Smith have been emulated in the Royal Fez Moroccan Tarot, the Mexican Tarot, the Aquarian Tarot and the Morgan Greer Tarot. For those desiring a touch of fantasy, the Tarot of the Cat People by Karen Kuykendall, or the Daughters of the Moon Tarot by Ffiona Morgan may well appeal. Those of a romantic nature may feel drawn to The Tarot of Love (**3**). These decks are usually accompanied by explanatory booklets and are available at most esoteric outlets.

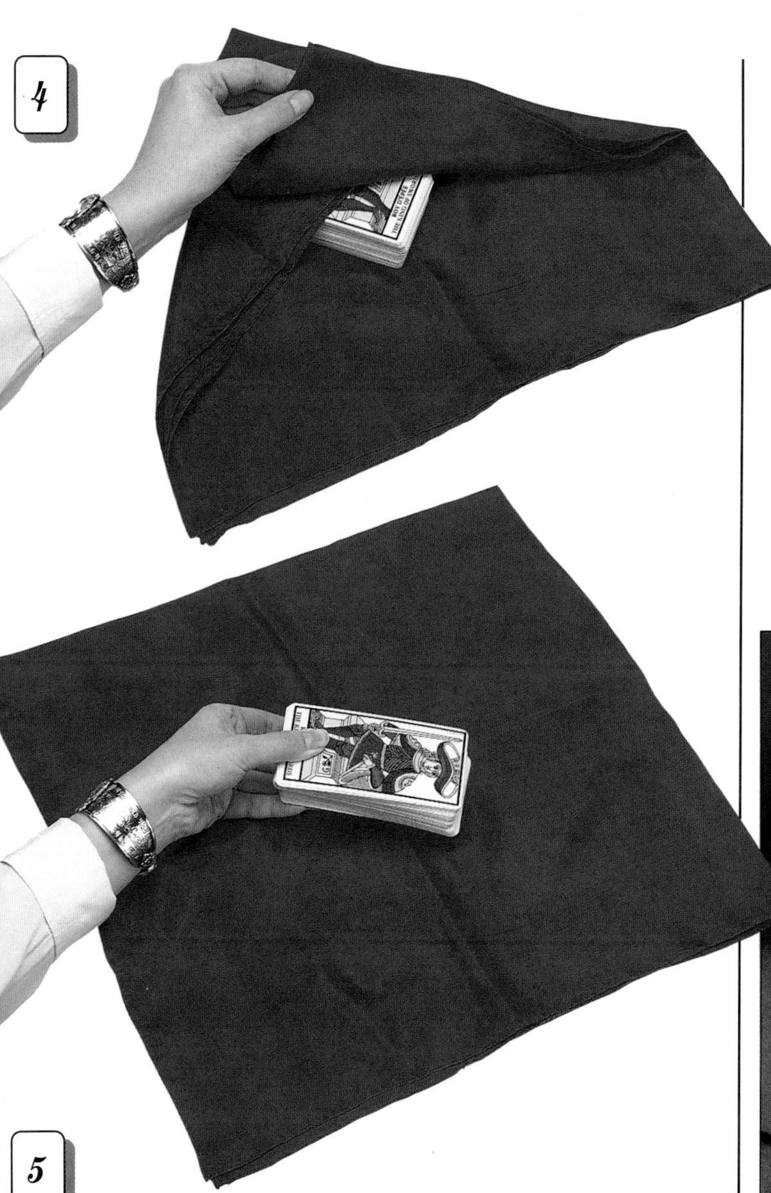

4

5

CARING FOR YOUR CARDS

Diviners generally keep their cards wrapped in a square of silk when not in use (**4**). Black silk is often used since this colour is said to repel evil influences. However, colour is a personal choice and most people have a favourite hue – one which gives them a sense of vibrancy and joy (**5**). If you are at ease with your choice, so too will be your cards.

When not in use, place your deck in a particular drawer, or a "special" wooden box or container which holds instant appeal for you. Centre your thoughts and you will intuitively know which "home" is best for your cards.

YOUR SPECIAL AURA

The Tarot is an extremely powerful, symbolic system and should be treated with all the respect that its arcane origin deserves. The cards are interpreted through the Diviner's natural gift of intuition, perception and a knowledge of the accumulated ancient wisdoms in the cards. It is, therefore, inadvisable to allow others to handle your cards as this destroys the *vital personal link* between yourself and your deck.

In order to strengthen the link between themselves and their cards, many Diviners sleep with them under their pillow at night, allowing the magic of the Tarot to infiltrate their inner psychic consciousness.

PREPARING TO DIVINE

Reading the Tarot is easier to do when you are in a state of relaxed concentration. This way you can interpret the cards more intuitively and with greater sensitivity. Prior to a reading or readings, the use of a simple relaxation exercise may be helpful. You may wish to develop your own method, but merely by breathing deeply and consciously dispelling negative, mundane influences for several minutes, an appropriate sense of calm can be induced.

CENTRE YOUR PSYCHIC ENERGY

With a state of calm achieved, slowly sift through the cards, looking at the face of each one, letting your imagination and inner consciousness dwell briefly on each, allowing a rapport to form between yourself and the cards (**1**). This exercise will stimulate your imaginative and psychic powers and the Tarot's exotic imagery will produce a kind of auto-hypnosis, at the same time enlivening your intuitive responses. The burning of a favourite incense or perfumed candle, or providing a background of appropriate music, may also assist you to achieve the right mood.

1

2

SHUFFLING THE CARDS

Each Diviner has his or her own way of shuffling the cards. Briskly, using two hands simultaneously (**2**) is one of the more positive ways of keeping energies alive and flowing. It is better than, for instance, holding the deck in the left hand and loosely dropping the cards in with the right, thereby allowing the deck's energy to disperse. This method is also inadvisable because the Enquirer can see the face of the cards. It is better that this does not happen until the Diviner turns them over, so that the Enquirer does not impose his or her own energy onto the cards thereby allowing the esoteric element to be retained until the actual reading. By developing and preserving a special ritual when shuffling and turning up the cards, you will preserve your own unique approach to your readings.

MYSTIC MOOD

In order to maintain your concentration, it is best not to make conversation with the Enquirer before the reading, except to ask them to cut the deck or to select a significator, if necessary (see right). Thereafter, keep your flow of energy sharp and clear, answer the questions of the Enquirer as you will, but try not to encourage chatty, mundane conversation.

The Tarot is read or interpreted by stimulating the psychic powers within each Diviner. It follows, therefore, that no two readings will be alike. The normal and reversed meanings of the cards are comparatively standard. However, from cards shuffled at random, each spread placed forms a special and magical link between the Enquirer and the unseen and is interpreted through the perceptive powers of the Diviner. The cards can point the way. They can offer advice but ultimately the Enquirer must make up his or her mind how best to deal with a given situation.

THE SIGNIFICATOR

A significator represents a person or object implying or expressing a special or hidden meaning. If required in a spread, the significator may be selected by the Diviner and will generally represent the Enquirer (**3**). The four suits symbolize the following: Clubs, a fair person with blue eyes; Cups, light brown hair and pale eyes; Swords, brown hair and brown eyes; Coins, black hair and dark eyes. For a man, the King of the appropriate suit is selected and for a woman, the Queen. For a young man, The Knight and for a young girl or child, the Page. The Enquirer may also be asked to select a significator simply by cutting the deck or by choosing a card from a selection proffered by the Diviner (**4**).

3

4

THE TAROT READING

The twenty-two pictorial cards of the Major Arcana are generally deemed by most Diviners to be adequate for their requirements. The *Tarot de Marseille* deck has been used to illustrate this book and shown in numerical sequence below (**1**) are the twenty-one numbered cards of the Major Arcana. The unnumbered card, The Fool, is positioned above. The Fool is a "wild" card and can take the place of any other, bringing an element of surprise and unexpected influence to a spread!

2

1

THE QUESTION IS PUT

Taking the cards from their protective wrapping, the Diviner encourages the Enquirer to ask his or her question. With regard to the type of question asked, the Diviner then decides upon an appropriate spread, shuffles the deck thoroughly and cuts the cards according to personal preference.

Shuffling may be by the hand over hand method (**2**), by riffling with the thumbs to intermix the deck (**3**) or by any other preferred method which is brisk and business-like. The reasons for this were explained in the **Preparing to Divine** section on pages 46-47.

Shuffling and cutting by the Diviner completed, the Enquirer is then asked to cut the cards once, using the left hand (**4**). This may be to select the significator or simply to impart the Enquirer's personal energy to the deck. If a significator is sought, this then will be at the bottom of the cut deck (**5**), to be brought out and read by the Diviner at an appropriate time. A significator may also be selected by the Diviner, or chosen from a fan of cards proffered to the Enquirer. This stage completed, the Diviner proceeds to turn over the cards, which are held in the left hand, with the right hand (**6**).

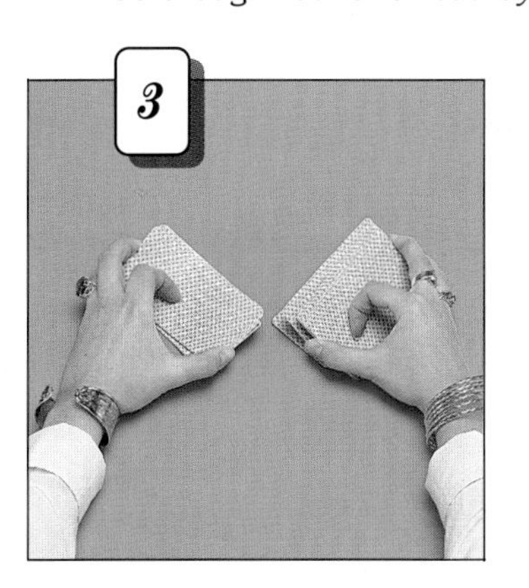
3

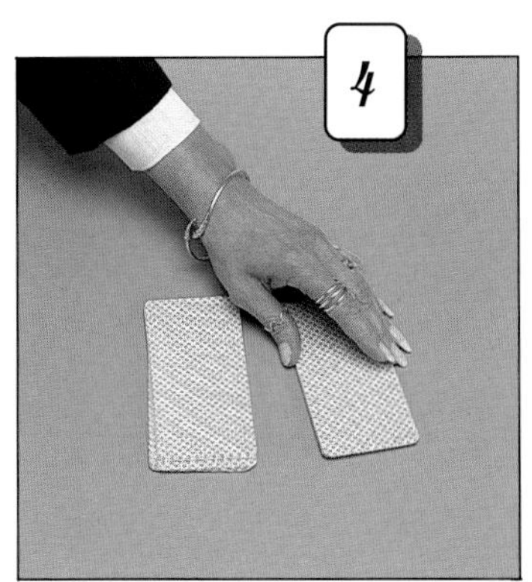
4

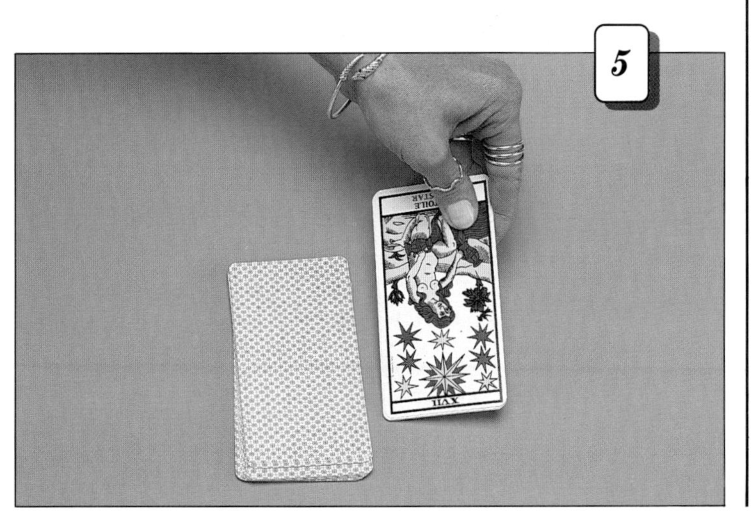
5

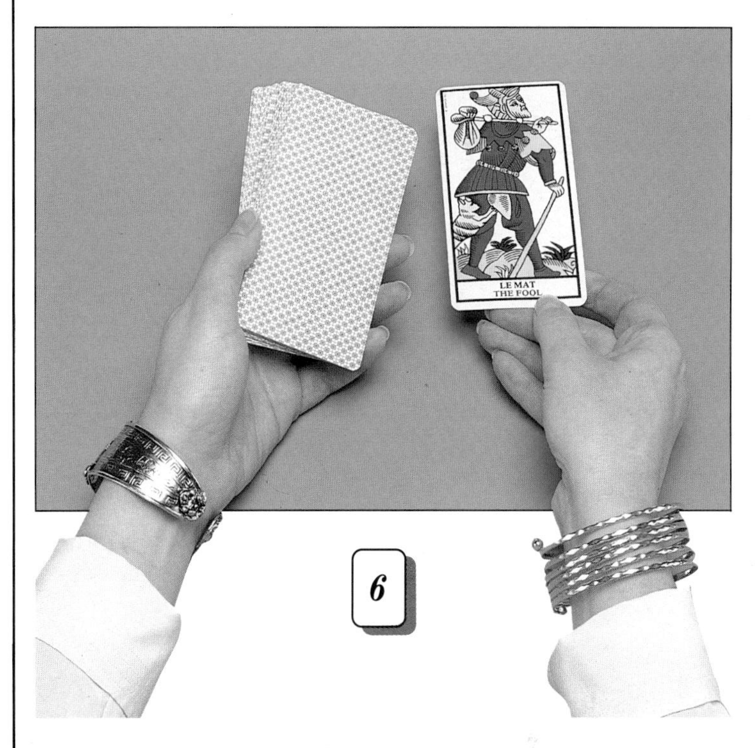

6

THE CELTIC CROSS

In this example imagine that the Enquirer's question is *"I have lost all direction to my life. Please give me some guidance."* The most appropriate spread to answer the Enquirer's question would be the all-encompassing Celtic Cross. Continue to turn over the cards from left to right as shown on the previous page. Cards facing the Diviner generally give strong, positive readings. Cards reversed or facing the Enquirer can hold weak or negative meanings.

SPREADING THE CELTIC CROSS

Position card one and place card two horizontally across it (**1**). Place card three above and card four below (**2**). Place card five to the left and card six to the right (**3**). Cards seven, eight, nine and ten are positioned vertically, far right (**4**).

The completed Celtic Cross spread should look like this (**5**). The meaning of each card in the Celtic Cross spread can be summarized as follows. One: Present conditions. Two: Obstacles ahead. Three: What is above you (future). Four: What is beneath you (passing out of your life). Five: What is behind you (past). Six: What is before you (future event). Seven: Secret fears. Eight: Present environment and how others see the Enquirer. Nine: Inner self and hopes. Ten: The outcome.

An example of a detailed reading and interpretation of a Celtic Cross spread is given overleaf.

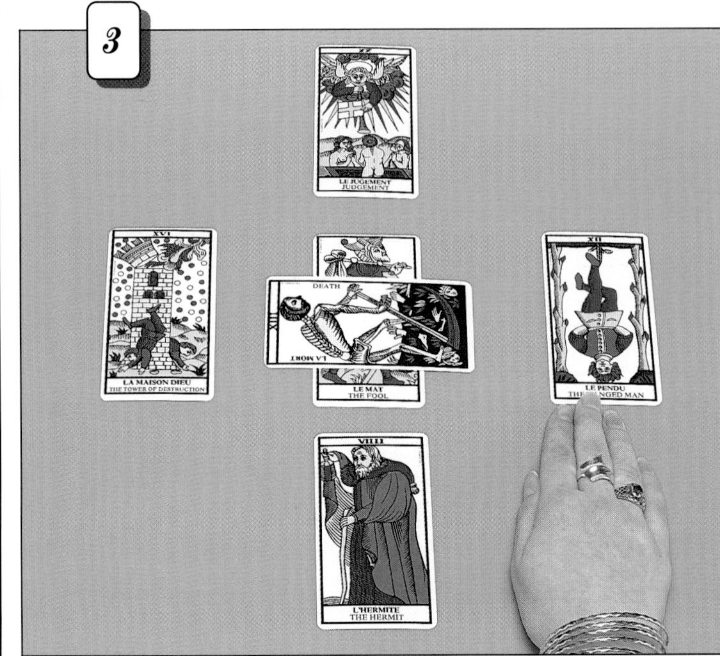

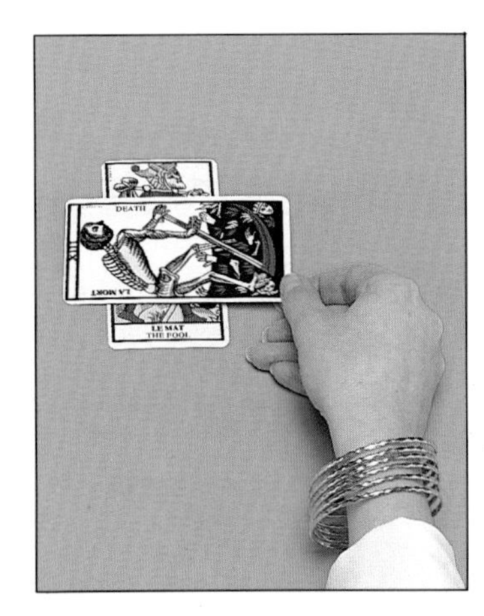

2

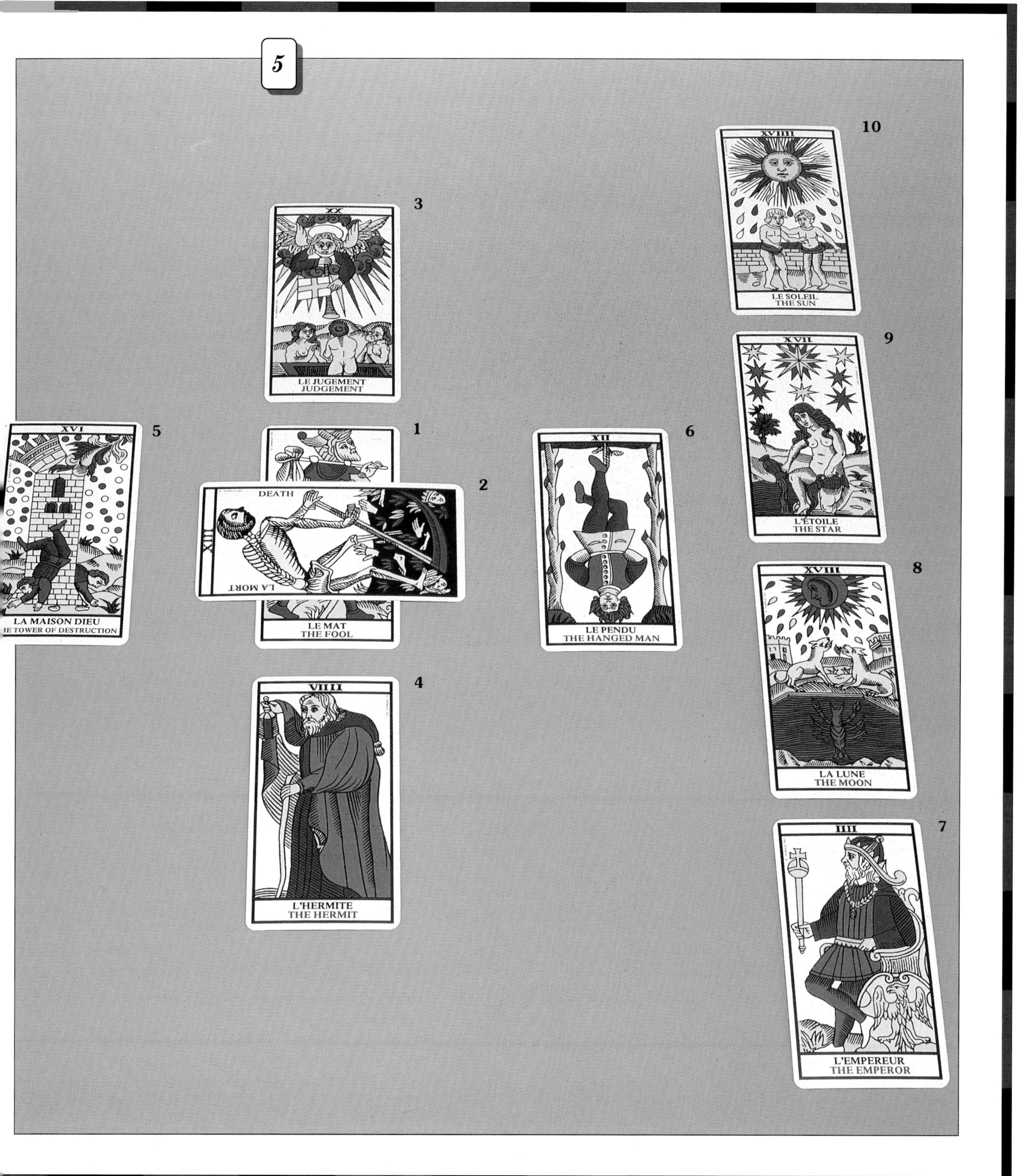
5
10
XVIIII
LE SOLEIL
THE SUN
3
XX
LE JUGEMENT
JUDGEMENT
9
XVII
L'ÉTOILE
THE STAR
5
XVI
LA MAISON DIEU
IE TOWER OF DESTRUCTION
1
2
DEATH
XIII
LA MORT
LE MAT
THE FOOL
6
XII
LE PENDU
THE HANGED MAN
8
XVIII
LA LUNE
THE MOON
4
VIIII
L'HERMITE
THE HERMIT
7
IIII
L'EMPEREUR
THE EMPEROR

THE CELTIC CROSS READING

The Celtic Cross lay-out and what the positions represent.

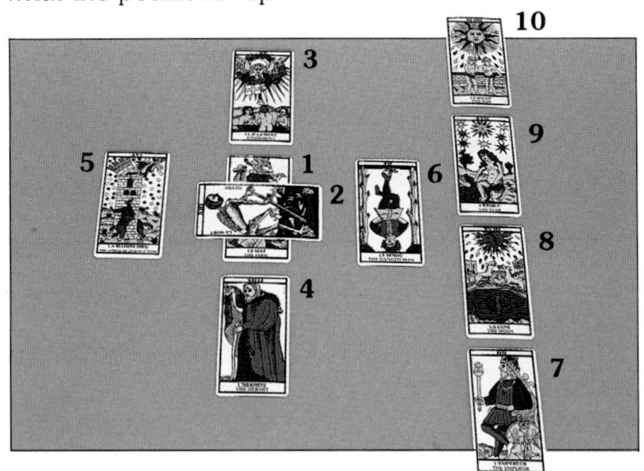

The Enquirer, Alice, is a 50-year-old former schoolteacher. Her husband has recently died and Alice has retired due to stress-related problems. Alice's grown-up son and daughter both live away from home and she feels isolated and trapped in her loneliness.

Card 1: The Fool 0. Present conditions

Alice is wandering aimlessly through life although The Fool suggests that she is doing so with a measure of hope and optimism. Now with few responsibilities, Alice is willing to make the most of her life, but does not know which direction to take . . .

Card 2: Death XIII. Obstacles ahead

Though the death of Alice's husband is there, it is not of physical death that this card speaks. It reflects the constant obstacles blocking the pathway of Alice's life, putting an end to every regenerative thought. No wonder Alice is so depressed.

Card 3: Judgement XX. What the future holds

Yet there is rebirth and regeneration in Alice's future. But first she must learn to accept her circumstances and to "forgive" herself for losing hope, for succumbing to desolation and self-pity. This she must do if she is to move forward.

Card 4: The Hermit VIIII. What Alice is leaving behind

Alice has journeyed alone. She has borne her burden and searched for the reasons behind the traumas she has recently experienced. She has felt desertion and loneliness in the extreme and in desperation has probably sought spiritual help and advice.

Card 5: The Tower of Destruction XVI. What is past

Alice's life has been devastated; comfortable domestic values have broken down and are destroyed. She has lost emotional security; a loving marital relationship has ended. Alice was in total despair, but a new order will arise out of her personal chaos.

Card 6: The Hanged Man XII. What lies directly ahead

Though unaware of this, Alice is on the road to recovery. She makes a conscious choice to face her problems; to look at them from a different angle and come to terms with them. Alice is gaining the strength to face the future.

Card 7: The Emperor IIII. Secret fears

Alice's secret fears are of facing life without the supportive presence of her husband; without his warmth, love, patience and wisdom. But Alice herself must bring that balance to her life. She should engender the powers of reason and logic, discipline and self-control.

Card 8: The Moon XVIII. Alice's present life and how others see her

Dreaming of yesteryear is a reality for Alice. Children and friends despair of her emotional escapism and self-deception. In order to make progress, she should approach life more positively.

Card 9: The Star XVII. Inner self and hopes

Symbolizing hope, renewal and inspiration, the Star could not have arrived at a more propitious moment for Alice. It offers light where there was darkness; replenishment where there was emptiness. Alice's cherished hopes and dreams are about to be realized.

Card 10: The Sun XVIIII. The outcome

This most fortunate of cards promises that, finally, Alice's dark journey is over. Her life will hold joyous new meaning and fulfilment. Energy and emotional and physical strength are boundless. Achievement, success, the promise of health, happiness and material stability are all present. And perhaps a new partner?

Summary: Following desolation and isolation there is hope, optimism and the promise of a brighter future for Alice. The cards have outlined the stages of her emotional insecurity and sense of aimlessness but, in their wisdom, they foretell joyful rebirth and regeneration – if Alice chooses to heed their advice.

THE BIRTHPATH SPREAD

One of the most personal aspects of an individual is their date of birth and it is fascinating to juggle with the numerology of an Enquirer's birthdate. In the Birthpath Spread the Enquirer can be sure that the message of the Tarot is for them alone, since this spread involves cards placed to the numeric value of their particular birthdate. In this instance, the Enquirer's birthdate is 26th April 1968, giving: 2 + 6 + 4 + 1 + 9 + 6 + 8 = 36. 3 + 6 = 9. The Birthpath number is, therefore, Nine. Nine cards are used and placed as shown (**1**).

INTERPRETING THE SPREAD

Representing a personal "biography" and also future trends in respect of the Enquirer, the cards are placed in three rows of three, left to right for each row in turn. Row 1 represents past influences; Row 2, present influences and Row 3, future influences.

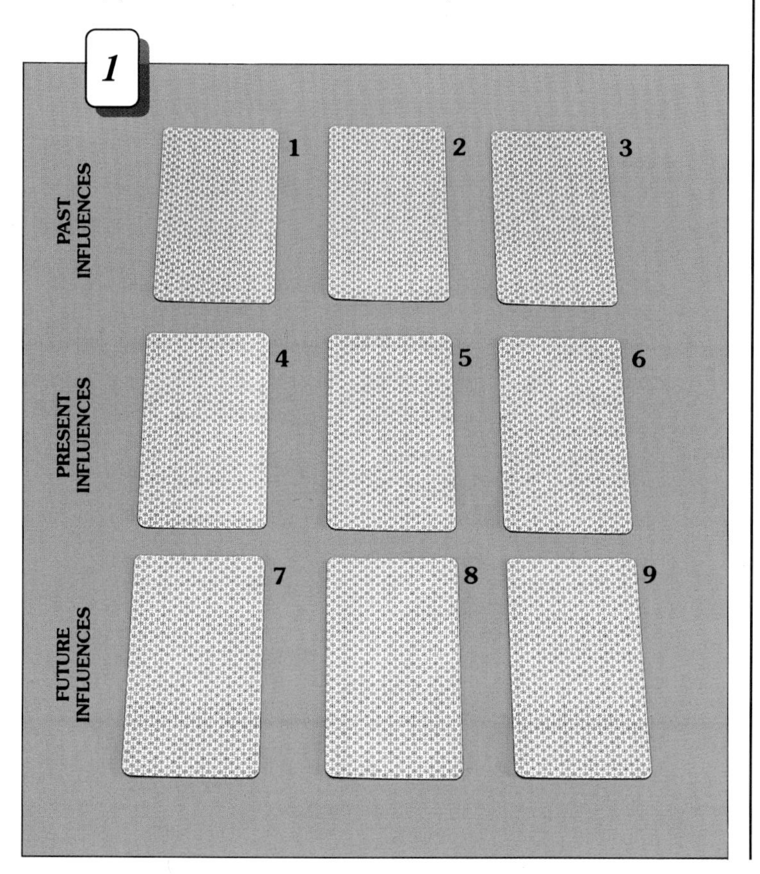

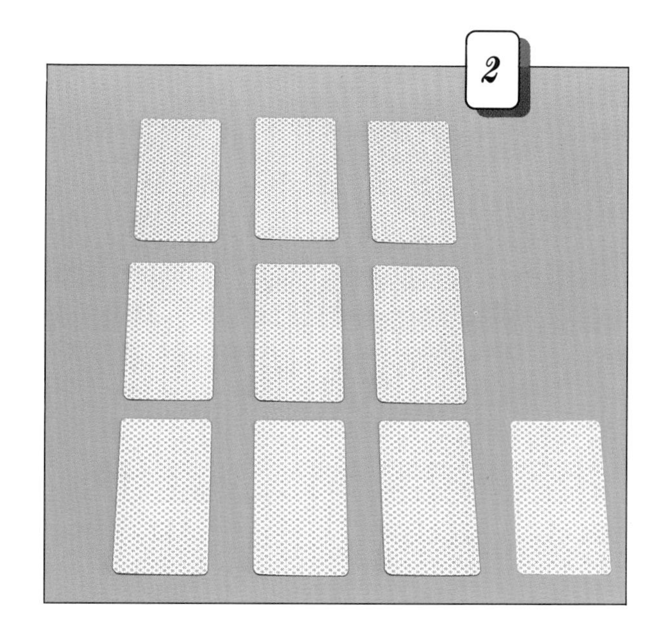

When I first originated this spread, I used the Major Arcana but found these cards to be inappropriately powerful. The Minor Arcana, including the court cards, is ideal, giving an indication of events in the "biography" and also of personalities met along the way.

Given that some birthdates can yield numbers of a lower value than 9, i.e. the 1st January 1972 equals a final number of 3, or 1st January 1955 equals a final number of 4, the number of letters in the month of birth should be calculated, i.e. January = 7. This number is then placed in lieu of the original "1" representing the month of birth.

The Birthpath number of 1st January 1972 is now 9 (1 + 7 + 1 + 9 + 7 + 2 = 27. 2 + 7 = 9) and the Birthpath number of birthdate 1st January 1955 is now 10 (1 + 7 + 1 + 9 + 5 + 5 = 28. 2 + 8 = 10). Additional cards in excess of 9 should be placed on Row 3 (Future Influences) (**2**). The Diviner then reads the cards accordingly.

The court cards represent:

King:	Authority
Queen:	Stability
Knight:	Assertiveness
Knave:	Receptiveness

Kings and Queens generally represent actual people or aspects of the Enquirer. Knights and Knaves often indicate events. See pp 25-41 for Minor Arcana interpretations and also Mystical Meanings on pp 42-43 for additional information on interpreting the Minor Arcana.

THE ZODIAC SPREAD

David, a 25-year-old musician is anxious to make the big time. He gets along quite well with other members of his group, but feels he will succeed more quickly if he goes solo. David asked: "*What do the next twelve months hold for me?*"

AN ASTROLOGICAL CONNECTION

Using the Major Arcana and the court cards of the Minor Arcana, the Zodiac Spread is perhaps the most appropriate for David's question, since it deals with the seasonal stages of the year ahead. This spread may also be interpreted through the solar transits, or the progressive signs of the zodiac. Only a basic knowledge of astrology is required to do this; for instance, simply knowing the sequence of Sun signs from Aries through to Pisces and their respective periods of duration is sufficient, i.e. Aries: 21st March - 20th April etc.

Shuffle the cards thoroughly and ask the Enquirer to cut the deck once, using his left hand and cutting to the right (**1**). From the top of the left-hand pile (pile one), take thirteen cards (**2**) and place them face down, in an oval formation (**3**), starting in a position just under your left hand and working in an anti-clockwise direction (**4**,**5**). Fan the remaining

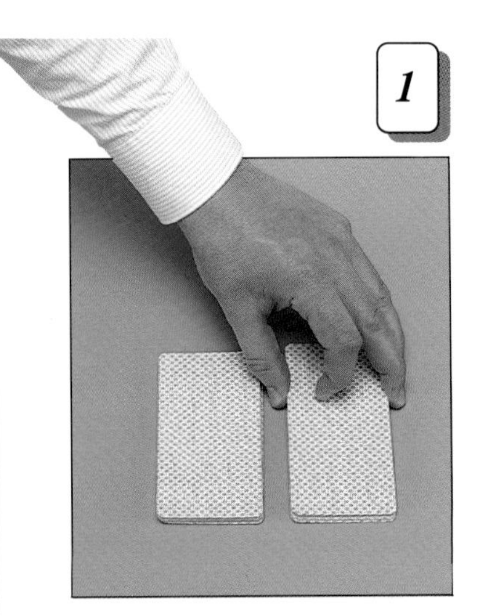

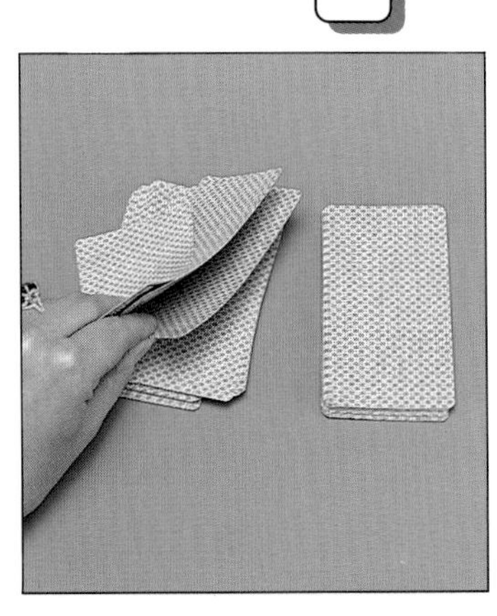

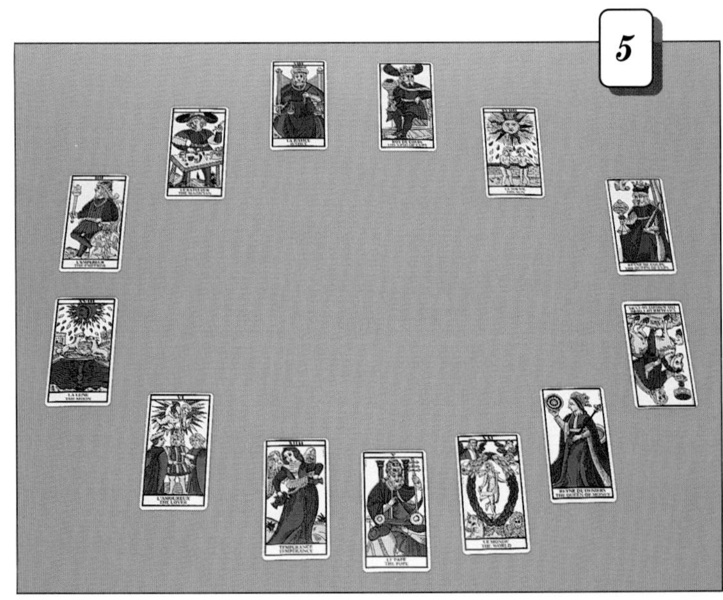

cards from pile one and ask the Enquirer to select one card (**6**). This is Significator One and represents the Enquirer for the twelve months ahead. Request that the Enquirer places this card, face up, in the centre of the spread (**7**). Read (interpret) this card. Take the bottom card from pile two of the cards cut by the Enquirer. This is Significator Two and symbolizes the energies surrounding the Enquirer for the coming twelve months. Read this card and place it, face up, across the card in the centre of the spread (**8**).

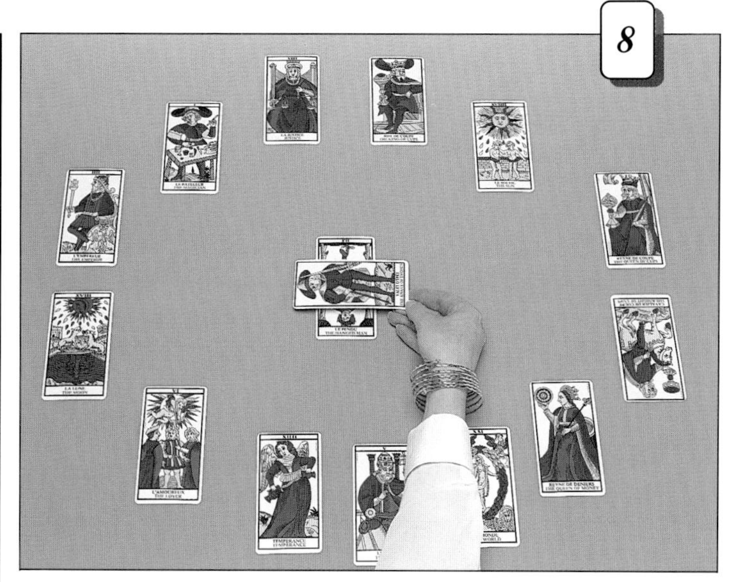

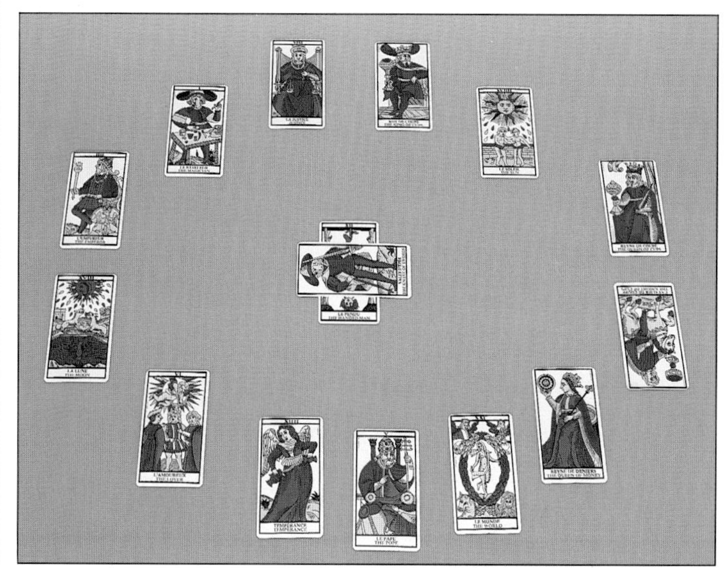

Significator One: The Hanged Man, representing David for the year ahead, indicates a serious attempt by the Enquirer to consider every aspect of his dilemma. *Significator Two:* The Knave of Swords represents the prevailing external energies encircling David over the next twelve months and warns of deception and malicious gossip.

READING THE ZODIAC SPREAD

Each group of cards illustrated represents the four seasons and relevant Sun signs as they progress through the year: Spring: Aries, Taurus and Gemini (**1**). Summer: Cancer, Leo and Virgo (**2**). Autumn: Libra, Scorpio and Sagittarius (**3**). Winter: Capricorn, Aquarius and Pisces (**4**). Card Thirteen represents the outcome. David asked his question in early March and so commenced with a Spring (Aries: 21st March - 20th April) reading. The seasonal groups however, are adjusted according to the time of year when the question is asked. For instance, a question asked in late July (Summer) would commence with the Leo: 23rd July - 23rd August section of Summer, working then through Autumn, Winter and Spring. Representing The Outcome, card Thirteen will be in the Spring section since this marks the end of David's twelve-month cycle.

Turn up the first three cards. These cards represent the immediate three months of the Enquirer's future. Starting with the Significators, read the cards and work through the remaining sections in this way:

Significator One: The Hanged Man is an appropriate card to represent David who is looking at his options from all angles and seeking new insight into the question of which direction to take.

Significator Two: The Knave of Swords representing David's surrounding energies over the next twelve months indicates that a brown-haired young girl could be deceitful or that, generally, he should beware of back-stabbing, rumour and gossip.

Spring: Card One: Temperance XIIII.

Aries: 21st March-20th April

Initially, David needs to acquire a balance and the wisdom to enable him to adapt and modify when confronted by change.

2

L'EMPEREUR THE EMPEROR 4

LE BATELEUR THE MAGICIAN 5

LA JUSTICE JUSTICE 6

SUMMER

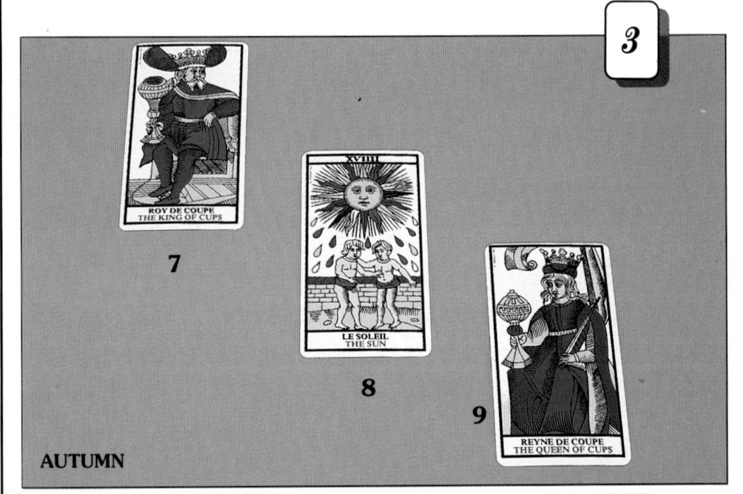

Card Two: The Lover VI.
Taurus: 21st April-21st May
There is either the possibility of a romance or there is a strong yearning for something more than David already has. Something that would bring all the trappings of material wealth. There is much indecision but also the beginnings of a firm resolve.
Card Three: The Moon XVIII.
Gemini: 22nd May-21st June
David dreams of becoming a star but he must beware of illusions and self-deception – also of false friends. David's dreams could be used to advantage; the mystic Moon could bring magic to his creative work. Forward planning needs to be as adept as he can make it.
Summer: Card Four: The Emperor IIII.
Cancer: 22nd June-22nd July
David is more determined than ever to go it alone. But he is also feeling cautious and applying reason and logic to his plans. He displays a strength of purpose he did not know he possessed.
Card Five: The Magician I.
Leo: 23rd July-23rd August
A doubling up of the magical "one" – the number common to both The Magician and Leo! With agility and alacrity, David has many plates in the air and is pulling lots of rabbits out of hats! Things are happening for him and he is full of confidence for the future. All the world promises to be a stage for David!
Card Six: Justice VIII.
Virgo: 24th August-22nd September
Wise choices could be made at this time. Legal matters are also indicated. He is reminded that mistrust and deception combine in his prevailing energies for the year. Damaging slander leads to a lawsuit?
Autumn: Card Seven: The King of Cups.
Libra: 23rd September-23rd October
The end of a phase and a new one begins. David meets a man of great compassion and artistic merit, bringing to David's life a spiritual awareness which is reflected in his music. This man is a powerful influence enabling David to relate insightfully to his inner feelings.
Card Eight: The Sun XVIIII.
Scorpio: 24th October-22nd November
David plumbs the depth of his artistic soul. The new relationship or partnership holds the promise of achievement, success and material rewards. Creativity abounds. There is joy, hope and optimism.
Card Nine: The Queen of Cups.
Sagittarius: 23rd November-21st December
A fair-haired woman who is charming, a good friend and is highly artistic, arrives on the scene. She could have a strong psychic ability. The wife or partner of the charismatic man David met during Libra's transit? Influenced by both, David's future holds the promise of truly great success.
Winter: Card Ten: Knight of Cups (reversed).
Capricorn: 22nd December-20th January
An untrustworthy person makes an appearance. Could it be the return of the brown-haired young girl? Perhaps even a rival in love. There is trickery afoot and emotional insecurity.
Card Eleven: The Queen of Coins.
Aquarius: 21st January-18th February
Regardless, David makes progress. There is material security; emotional and physical wellbeing and the trappings of luxury which he so desires. There could be a generous woman friend who is helpful in a practical way.
Card Twelve: The World XXI.
Pisces: 19th February-20th March
There is now fulfilment of David's desires. Eleven months of tough decisions, trials and tribulations and much hard work have culminated in David having reached his final goal. His joy – and his year – are complete. He has made it!
The Outcome: The Pope V
Following the achievement of material wealth and creative fulfilment, the luxurious lifestyle accompanying David's mercurial rise to fame was the ultimate reward. Or was it? David is destined to value a more meaningful, even conventional way of life, winning the whole-hearted approval of family and friends. He will gain a deeper inner wisdom, realizing that there is more to life than the accumulation of worldly goods. David will also find that his music will be correspondingly sincere, as will the warmth of his public acclaim.

THE TREE OF LIFE

The Tree of Life is one of the most arcane methods of reading life's full history. This spread undertakes to summarize the entire lifetime up to the present of the Enquirer. It also encompasses his or her hopes and fears for the future. The Tree of Life need only be read once in twelve months for any Enquirer, as it is unlikely that events will have progressed or changed significantly during that time to justify a second reading. To accommodate the wide-ranging scope of this spread the entire 78-card deck of the Tarot has been used.

PREPARING THE CARDS

Because the Tree of Life is so irrevocably entwined with the past, present and future of the Enquirer, he or she is asked to project their energy onto the cards by shuffling the deck. While doing so, the entire spectrum of their life up to the present should be swiftly envisaged, as should expectations and fears for the future. Using the left hand, the Enquirer cuts the cards twice and places them to the left, producing three piles in all (**1**). Each of the piles is passed to the Diviner (**2**) who then lays them out in the order shown (**3**). The cards are taken in sequence from each of the three piles, as is explained below.

THE MEANING OF THE SPREAD

Triangle One (cards 1, 2 and 3) represents the Spirit.
Triangle Two (cards 4, 5 and 6) represents Reason.
Triangle Three (cards 7, 8 and 9) represents the Unconscious.

Card Ten represents the Enquirer's physical self or earthly home.

The principles, or meanings of the numbers, in the Tree of Life spread can be summarized as follows:

1 The Enquirer's spiritual life at its highest peak.
2 The primal creative force (father/masculine).
3 The fountain of life (mother/feminine).
4 The virtues.
5 Intellectual and/or physical powers.
6 Health and temperament.
7 Desire, love and/or marriage (Venus card).
8 Children. The arts.
9 Imagination. Dreams and creative power.

The *vertical* rows in the spread represent the Branches of the Tree of Life. The Branch of Discipline lies to the left; the Branch of Harmony is in the centre and the Branch of Love is to the right.

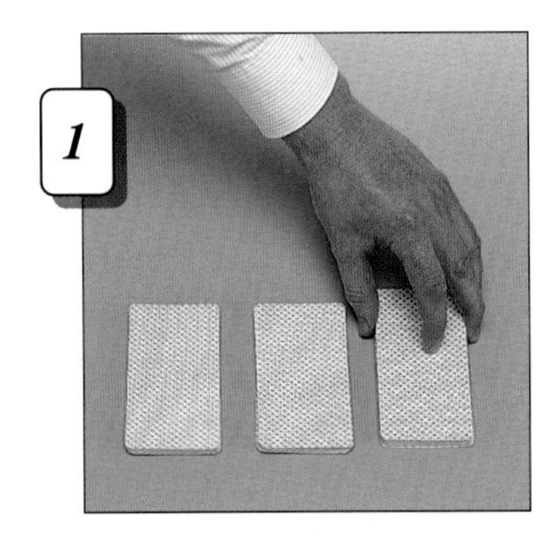

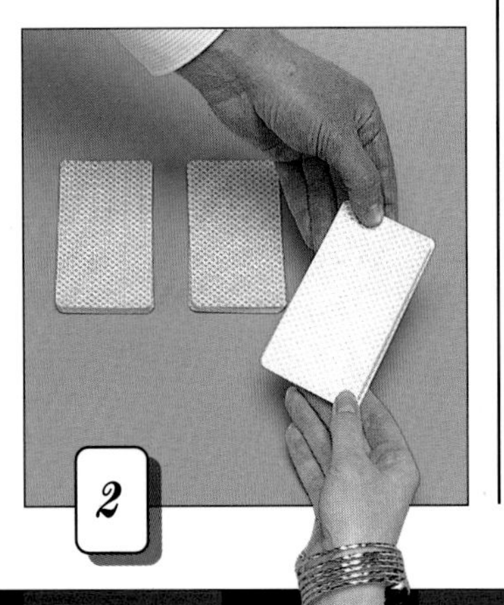

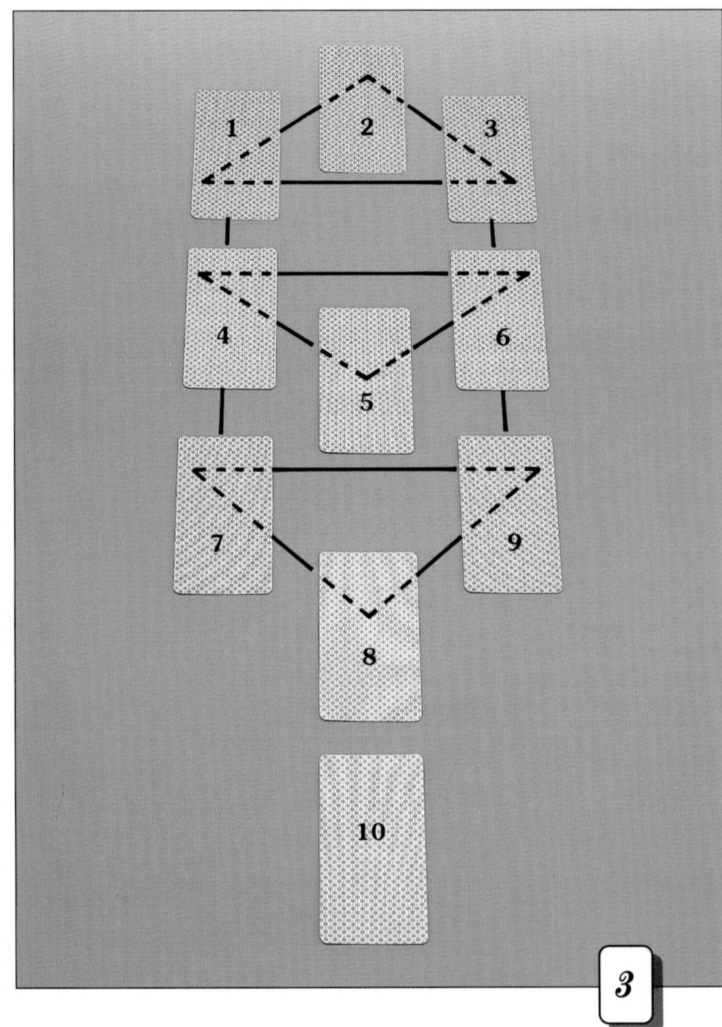

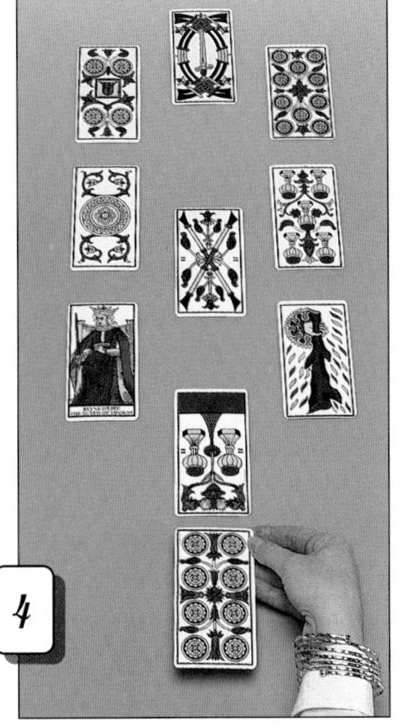

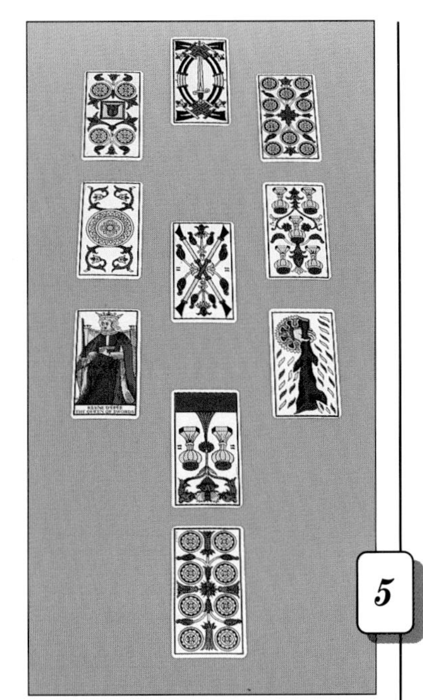

METHOD OF LAYING THE TREE OF LIFE SPREAD

The Diviner lays down the cards, face up. The first three cards come from pile one; the second three from the top of pile two and the third three from the top of pile three. All are placed in the order shown on the opposite page. The tenth card is then taken from the top of pile three and is placed in position (**4**,**5**). The Diviner shuffles the remaining cards and deals out the first seven cards, face down (**6**). These cards will be read when the other cards have been interpreted; they represent the unrealized dreams of the Enquirer's immediate future (**7**).

THE TREE OF LIFE SPREAD READING

The Enquirer is 30-year-old Paul who is single and a bank clerk.

Triangle One (Cards 1, 2 and 3): The spiritual self
The Earthy presence of Coins in this section indicates that Paul could have an obsession with material wealth and that this is reflected in his dealings with others and life generally. The Five of Swords suggests that this attitude is rebounding on Paul, who is disliked and has few friends. Paul sees the error of his ways! The accent again is on material security; a stable home life and family values. Perhaps the Ten of Coins dropped by to remind Paul just how rich life *could* be for him!

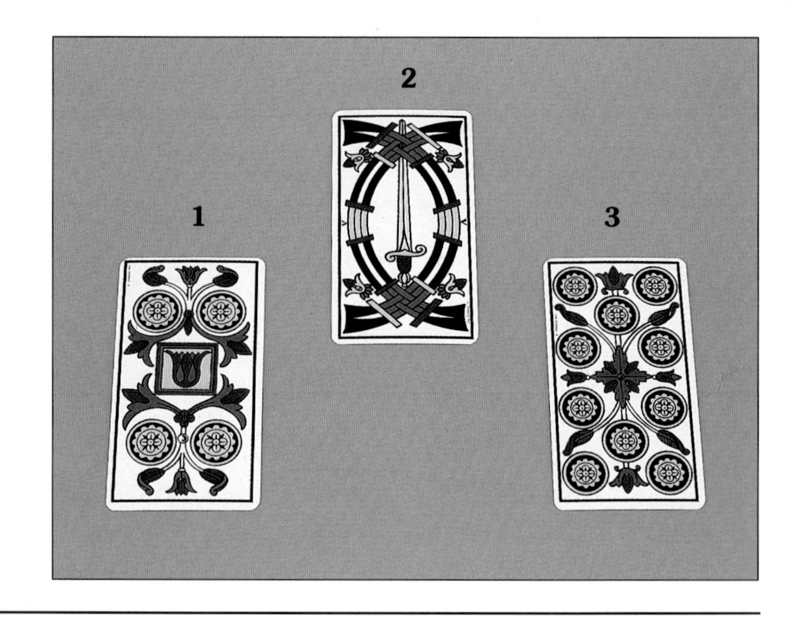

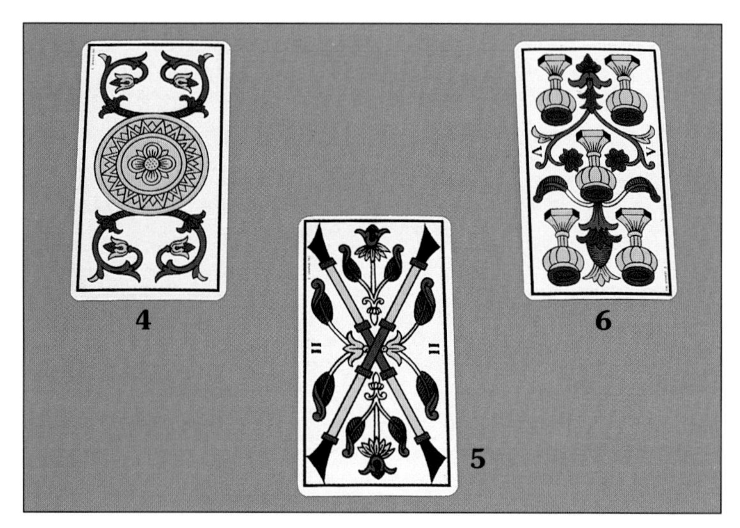

Triangle Two (Cards 4, 5 and 6): The father/masculine principle
Was Paul's father a dominant authority in his life? The indications are that this was so. The Ace of Coins suggests that Paul's father enjoyed the security and status of an astute business man. Was there a thriving family business in which, as a child, Paul had worked hard and long at his father's instigation? Perhaps a future partnership had been planned. The Two of Clubs, however, indicates that this particular potential remained unfulfilled; that there was restlessness, change and that, eventually, Paul chose to go his own way with eventually a favourable outlook, Five of Cups reversed.

Triangle Three (Cards 7, 8 and 9): The mother/feminine principle
The Queen of Swords indicates that Paul's mother was a shrewd, intelligent and articulate woman. Possibly widowed, she may have become increasingly withdrawn, distancing herself from her son Paul. The Two of Cups reversed suggests that Paul quarrelled or grew apart from his mother – probably the former since there is a degree of disharmony – subsequently falling into the wrong company. A downward trend appeared to follow, the Ace of Clubs reversed. Perhaps these new companions separated Paul from his wealth, giving him good reason to be cautious and prudent when dealing with others?

Card Ten: The physical self and earthly home
The Eight of Coins brings "skills improved by practice". Perhaps Paul will abandon his banking career and take up a craft or vocation at which he would excel. As Coins are an Earth suit, working with his hands with wood, clay or earth would be most appropriate. There are indications that this could lead to a much more spiritually and financially rewarding future for Paul.

THE 7-CARD PACK: IMMEDIATE FUTURE

Card One: The Empress (III) The Empress indicates that Paul will be successful in his choice of new career and that this will be both spiritually and materially rewarding as promised by the Eight of Coins. He will also meet a young woman with whom he will enjoy a happy and stable relationship.
Card Two: Five of Clubs This card indicates initial opposition from some quarter. Paul's mother, perhaps, in disagreement with his change of career? This problem will flare and quickly die down. There will be minor difficulties in most areas of life.
Card Three: Four of Swords There will be relief from Paul's anxieties. A time of productive solitude for the young couple is in order. Perhaps a holiday from which they will return refreshed and revitalized!
Card Four: Knave of Clubs This cheerful, impulsive card brings good news! Could this be the birth of a fair-haired child to Paul and his wife?
Card Five: Queen of Clubs There enters either a personable fair-haired woman, a formidable rival to others, or an indication of success for Paul's business. More likely the latter.
Card Six: King of Clubs Paul could meet a fair-haired man, clever, impulsive and an instant decision-maker. Perhaps a family member or a friend to help in the business in a marketing or sales capacity.
Card Seven: The High Priestess (II) Representing the intuitive aspect of self, Paul would appear to be ever more insightful in his attitude to his craft, his relationships with others and in his outlook generally. In his search for deeper spiritual enlightenment Paul may consider taking up studies of an occult nature.

SUMMARY

From his domineering, money-conscious father and the ultimately unsatisfactory relationship with his mother, Paul learned the negative aspects of material security and emotional insecurity. Aspects which subsequently blighted his relationships with others. In his three triangles, the presence of Coins, a Taurus suit governed by the element Earth, indicates an emphasis on the inbuilt Taurean awareness of possessions which, when over-stressed, can lead to avarice and meanness. A complete change of direction and a more balanced approach to life mean happiness and stability for Paul, culminating in an increasingly enlightened sense of spiritual awareness.

THE 5-CARD HORSE-SHOE SPREAD

This spread is ideal for an Enquirer who is at a cross-roads in life and requires to know the general trend of fortunes from the present through to the foreseeable future. Helen, single and 33 years old, has been made redundant from her position as Personal Assistant to a company MD. With her redundancy money, Helen wishes to start her own interior design company and asks if she would make a success of this new venture.

THE SPREAD IS LAID

Only Helen herself can ultimately determine this, but the cards *can* indicate key pointers. Giving a concise meaning to the nature of events, the Minor Arcana cards 1-10 inclusive are used for this spread (**1**).

Helen is asked to shuffle the forty Minor Arcana cards and return them to the Diviner who, with the left hand, turns up cards One to Five from the top of the deck and places them, face up and starting from the left (**2**). The Diviner is now able to see the Tarot's interpretation of Helen's present and future.

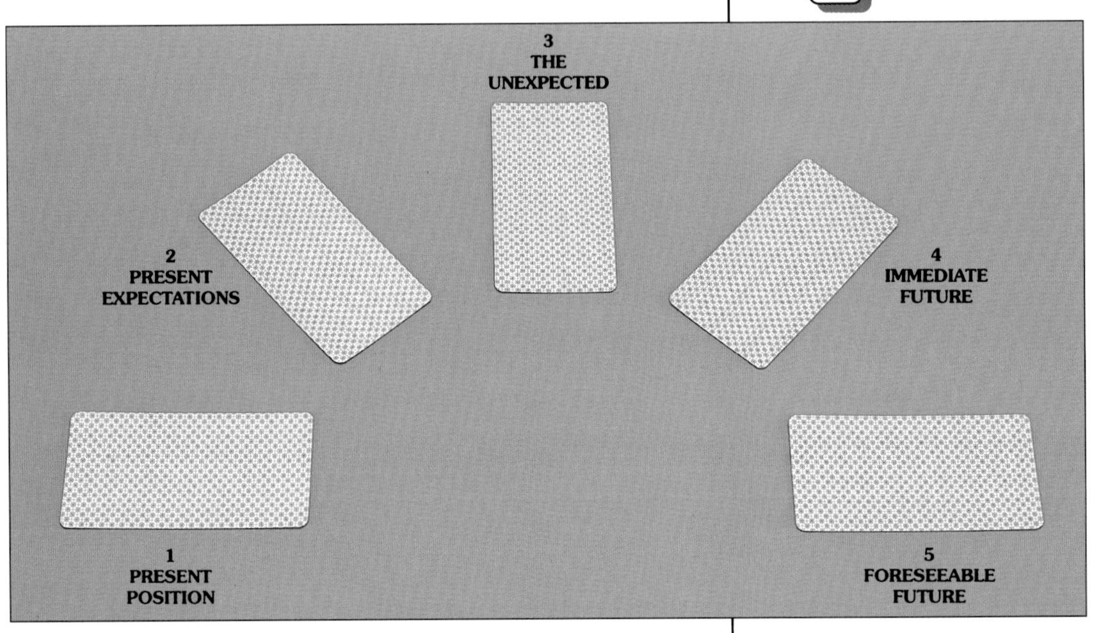

THE 5-CARD HORSESHOE SPREAD READING

Seeing the preponderance of Swords in Helen's reading, I was tempted to re-shuffle and start again, but intuitively felt that the cards, in their wisdom, had fallen that way for reasons best known to themselves. They indicated an unexpected slant on the outcome of Helen's proposed new career.

Card One: Seven of Swords. Present position
This card indicates that Helen is applying reason and logic in weighing up the pros and cons of her proposed project. Following much market research, mental debate and deliberation, she decides to go ahead with her plan.

Card Two: Ten of Swords. Present expectations
The end of an era for Helen. After her structured, well-ordered life at the office, she has a few reservations about the insecurity of self-employment, but bright new pastures beckon and it's on to the next stage of Helen's career.

Card Three: Nine of Swords. The unexpected
With the arrival of this comfortless card and, uncharacteristically in view of her earlier optimism, Helen experiences grave anxiety and concern for her new venture. Can she cope? What if it fails and all is lost?

Card Four: Two of Swords. Immediate future
Helen is due to find herself at a second crossroads with the appearance of something, or someone, new on the scene. The next card suggests a relationship or a serious romance. Plans are put on hold. Commitments are called for. Her career or her relationship? A decision must be made.

Card Five: Ten of Cups. Foreseeable future
The Ten of Cups promises the ultimate fulfilment of family life and all the joy that this implies. An "unforeseeable" outcome? Certainly, but if Helen heeds the message of the cards in her spread, she will be a happy and contented young woman. At some later stage in her life, family commitments permitting, Helen's dream of running her own interior decor company may yet come to fruition . . .

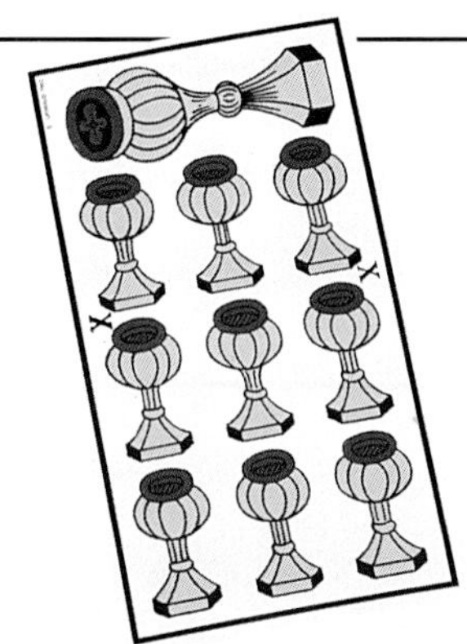

Additional points to note in Helen's reading:

- Card 3: The Nine of Swords can also mean "bad omen"
- Nine of Swords: Keyword meaning of Number 9: The power of the suit. Keyword meaning of Swords: The intellect. Strife. Difficulty.
- Ten of Cups: Keyword meaning of number 10: Perfection through completion. Consummation. End of the journey.
- The character of Cups: Feeling

Finally . . .

- In the fifth and final card of Helen's reading, a Cups card brings the message of a happy marriage and the fulfilment of family life.
- The numeric value of the five cards placed is: 7 + 10 + 9 + 2 + 10 = 38. 3 + 8 = 11. 1 + 1 = 2.
- Number Two: A balance of opposites, i.e. light/dark; positive/negative; male/female.
- Two in the Cups suit: An ideal balance of physical and spiritual love. Partnerships. Union. Harmony. This bodes extremely well for Helen's future happiness!

THE 7 PERSONAL PLANETS SPREAD

Many Tarot readers devise their own spreads and, having a particular interest in astrology, I devised the Seven Personal Planets Spread specifically to deal with problems of an immediate, personal nature. For instance: *"My boyfriend has asked me to marry him, yet something holds me back. Why?"* Or, *"I have the opportunity to be manager of our overseas office. There's an increase in salary, but I lack the confidence to take this step. What should I do?"* The Major Arcana is used for this spread as these cards bring the strongest, most powerful message.

THE PERSONAL PLANETS

Since we all have seven "personal" planets in our birth charts, this spread establishes a close relationship with the Enquirer and their individual problem. The Seven Personal Planets Spread may also be interpreted in the absence of the Enquirer and divination may be given in written form or verbally by telephone.

N.B. In a reading, the Tarot cards are the "prime movers". The planets are the influencing factors. For in-depth Major Arcana divinatory meanings see pp 12-24.

Number One card, The Sun, representing the Enquirer's own "Sun" sign will be the key card in the spread. The example illustrated showing The Magician in the Sun position suggests a person with agility of mind and movement and a degree of cunning. The seven planets placed in sequential order from left to right and their keywords are as follows:

1	☉	The Sun:	Power. Vitality.
2	☽	The Moon:	Instinctive reactions.
3	☿	Mercury:	Communications. Mentality.
4	♀	Venus:	Harmony. Relationships.
5	♂	Mars:	Energy. Drive.
6	♃	Jupiter:	Expansion. Maturity.
7	♄	Saturn:	Caution. Self-control.
8		The Outcome	

INTERPRETING THE SPREAD

For this sample interpretation, the first question has been used: *"My boyfriend has asked me to marry him yet something holds me back. Why?"*

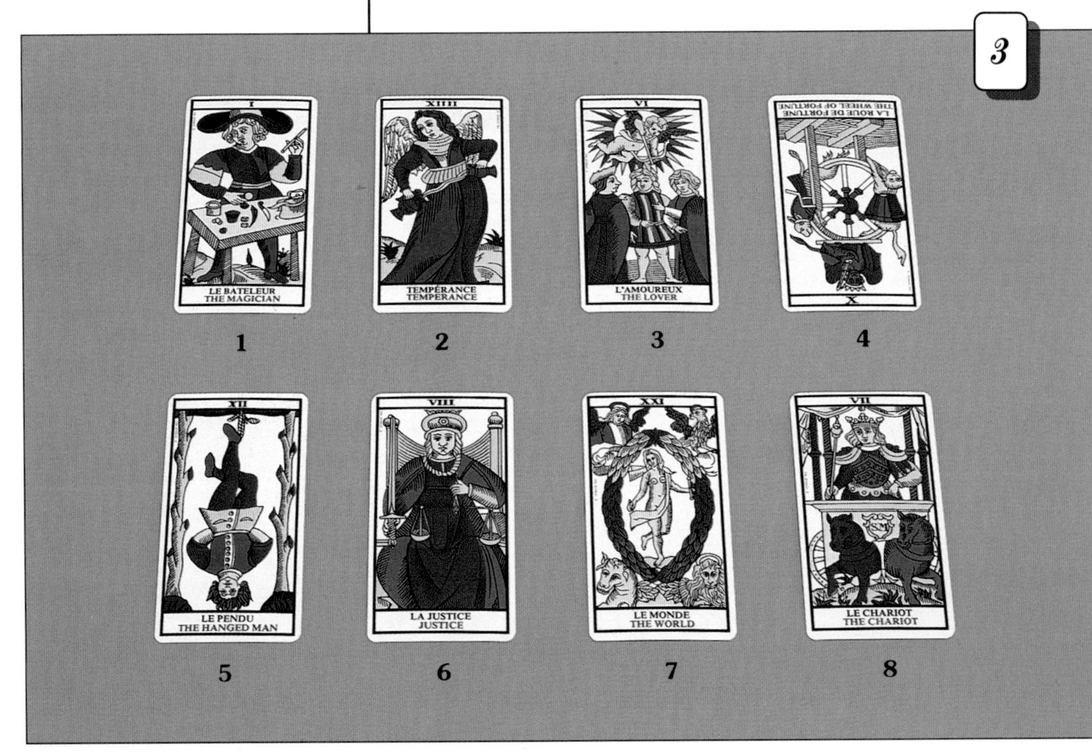

Shuffle the twenty-two cards of the major Arcana, then with the left hand take the first eight cards from the top of the deck and place as in the sequence shown (**1-3**). Bearing in mind the query, take the divinatory meanings of each card and apply the relevant planetary influences, respectively. A basic interpretation of the eight cards follows.

Card One: The Magician I Here is an ingenious individual; a young woman with great spontaneity of spirit and dextrous mental skills. She is self-assertive, not a little arrogant, and expresses herself with power and vitality (☉ *The Sun*).

Card Two: Temperance XIIII This card symbolizes successful union and stresses the wisdom of a balanced heart and the capacity to modify and adapt when confronted by change. ☽ *The Moon* urges the Enquirer to be more reflective and less arrogant in her instinctive reactions to life and everyday situations.

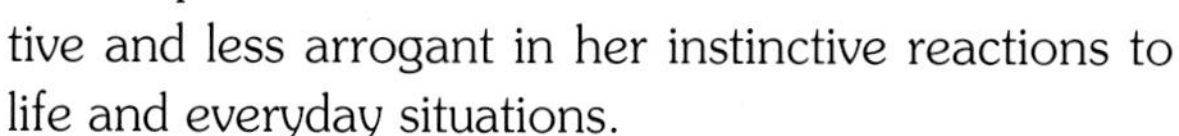

Card Three: The Lover VI Choices are to be made and ☿ *Mercury* emphasizes communications on a mental level.

Card Four: The Wheel of Fortune X (reversed) Expected events take an unexpected turn. Good fortune eludes and there is an inability to meet challenge. ♀ *Venus* puts the accent on relationships.

Card Five: The Hanged Man XII A search for the truth. Looking at the problem from a different, or someone else's, angle? ♂ *Mars* suggests that this exercise is carried through with energy and drive.

Card Six: Justice VIII This card is about making wise choices or decisions and adjusting to the situation following these. Reason transcends emotion. ♃ *Jupiter* implies that wisdom and maturity follows this stage.

Card Seven: The World XXI All previous trials and experiences culminate in this card. The Enquirer's final goal is reached; there is joy and a new life. Twenty-one is a fortunate card on which to end but a cautionary ♄ *Saturn* encourages discipline and self-control.

THE OUTCOME

Card Eight: The Chariot VII The Enquirer has learned that a middle course should be steered. A balance in all things is required. This journey, for her, has been accomplished.

It is seen that the Enquirer's original relationship with her boyfriend was satisfactory but with the question of marriage, doubts were raised in her mind (Card Two). Mercury suggests that the lovers were at odds, mentally. Perhaps their perception of a perfect partnership differed (Card Three)? Venus highlights the area of relationships; matters go seriously wrong and neither can cope with the situation (Card Four). An answer is vigorously sought (Card Five), but both wisely decide that they are not yet ready for a final commitment (Card Six). A decision is taken to learn from past experiences and to take matters slowly for the time being. Saturn urges caution and self control (Card Seven). Lessons have been learnt. The Enquirer herself, recognizes that she is not yet ready for marriage and perhaps needs to adopt a more philosophical view of life and a less insensitive attitude towards others. She may also discover that happiness lies not only in receiving, but also in giving.

The World celebrates the perfect integration and completion of a Whole which, in the Book of the Alchemists, symbolizes the completion of the Great Work. The Great Work is to bring ourselves and thereby the World into a state of Perfection . . .

PART TWO

CARTOMANCY

THE ORIGIN AND HISTORY OF CARTOMANCY

Cartomancy, or fortune-telling by playing cards, has been practised since ancient times. Historically it is linked with nomadic gypsies from Egypt and India who, wandering the Mediterranean area, travelled up through Spain and so north into the rest of Europe. To the Indians, the cards held a deep religious mysticism and for them, each suit was named after an incarnation of the god Krishna.

Fortune Telling, a romantic early Victorian notion of card prediction, as painted by Abraham Solomon (1824-62).

CULTURAL EXCHANGE

From the early 13th century, trade routes between the Mediterranean countries, Asia Minor and the Far East were established with the subsequent linkage of the various cultures and religions. Meanwhile, cartomancy became increasingly popular and widespread, as a method of foretelling the future.

The funeral of France's King Charles VI, in whose court playing cards initially gained much popularity.

That the Knights Templar, a military religious order founded by the Crusaders in Jerusalem around 1118 A.D., were responsible for bringing knowledge of the cards to Europe was most probable; they in turn learned about them from the Saracens during the Holy Land crusades. On their return to Europe, the Knights were known to have practised card games, since it is recorded to have met with some opposition from the Church.

It is said that, around 1390, King Charles VI of France became afflicted with severe bouts of mental depression and that to combat this his mistress introduced him to an exciting new game currently popular in Paris, recently having been brought there by gypsies. This game involved cards featuring numbers and images of various eastern kings and queens. On a whim, the King's mistress ordered the court artist to design cards depicting known members of the court, including the King himself, and of course, his mistress.

Thereafter known as the "court cards", the King was so highly delighted with them that he instantly regained his mental equilibrium and announced to one and all his recommendation of the cards, giving them the royal seal of approval. It was not until a wily gypsy provided the King with a prophetic reading of these cards that members of court began to

show their concern, as various plots, love-affairs and other nefarious activities were revealed. This finally led to the King being forced to ban the cards from use, both in the court and out of it.

In the mid-18th century, however, Frenchman Jean-François Aliette discovered that fortune-telling was a profitable business and, reversing his name to style himself Etteila, "the master of cartomancy", he published a book entitled *How to Amuse Oneself with a Pack of Cards*. In this book, Etteila developed a basic set of rules for the 32-card pack (see below).

The 52-card pack of playing cards is said to represent Time. The four suits symbolize the four seasons of the year; the twelve picture cards, the months of the year; and the fifty-two cards, the weeks of the year. The court or picture cards, King, Queen and Jack, symbolize the family – an older man, a mature woman and a young man or child. Traditionally, red cards, Hearts and Diamonds, are considered to be favourable, while black cards, Clubs and Spades, can signify ill luck, especially the latter suit.

Queen Anne playing cards depicting the military victories of the Duke of Marlborough.

The basic divinatory pack, however, is generally the 32-card deck, all cards being of seven or a higher value. Ace is high.

Above: The courageous resistance of the people, seen on the Eight of Spades card – one of a set of four depicting propagandist scenes from the Napoleonic wars.

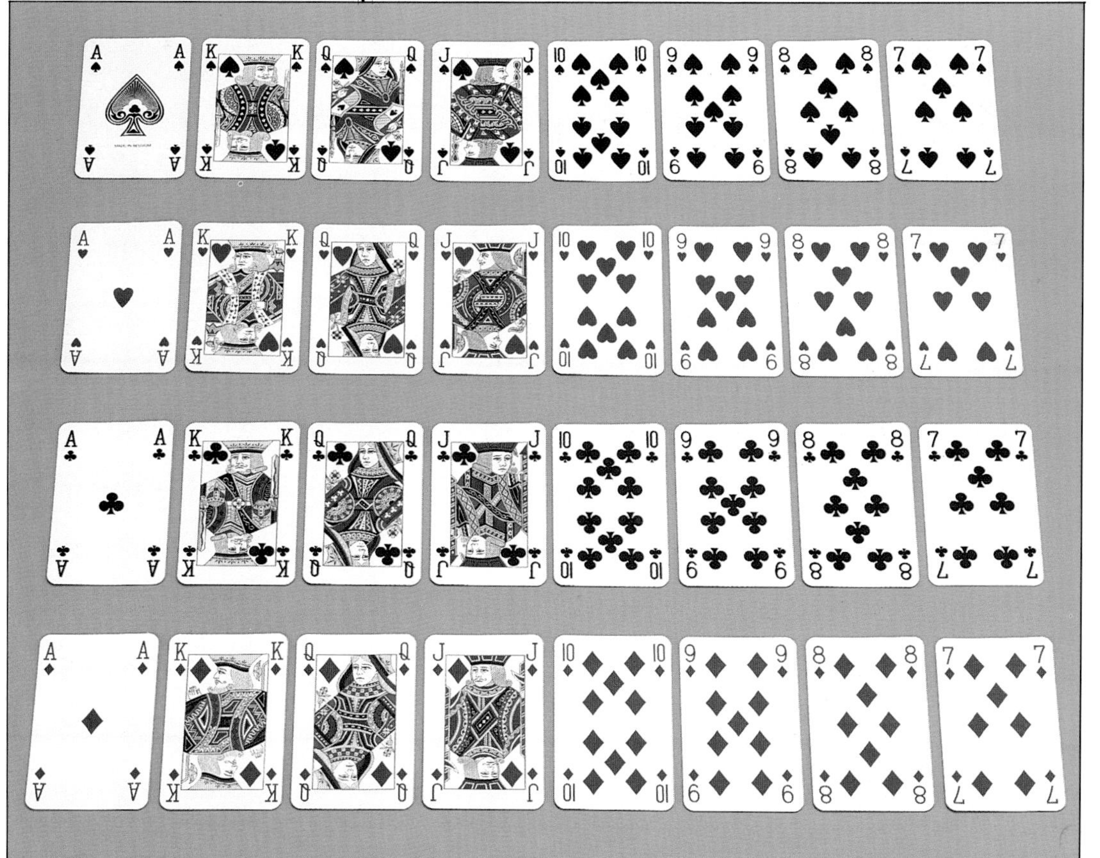

THE DECK AND ITS INTERPRETATIONS

On the previous page we saw that the 52-card deck of playing cards is said to represent Time and how the cards and suits correspond with the seasons, months and weeks of the year. The court cards of King, Queen and Jack constitute a fundamental "family" comprising an older man, a mature woman and a young man or child. The Jack may, on occasion, represent a young girl but, generally, the Queen represents all aspects or instances of a female. As the medieval court was said to symbolize the microcosm of Man, depicting the ideal social system to which all others should aspire, so the court cards represent a typical hierarchy comprising every type of person.

DUALISM IN THE CARDS

Red and black, the prevailing colours in the deck, symbolize duality in life and in our natures. While red playing cards generally signify a female or feminine attributes, black represents the male and masculine equivalents. All life reflects this duality and the reconciliation or balance of opposites is an essential factor in maintaining a necessary equilibrium in our lives.

There are 26 red cards and 26 black cards in the deck so that within its very make-up lies a basic balance. When the cards are shuffled and dealt to us, we each have the chance to play them to the best of our advantage. Again, the cards are a microcosm and we play our hand with them – in much the same way as with the cards dealt to us by Fate, in the broader game of Life – as best we can.

Above: Pegasus and Little Horse from a set of astronomically themed 18th century German playing cards.

Left: The Cheat with the Ace of Diamonds by the French painter Georges de la Tour (1593-1652).

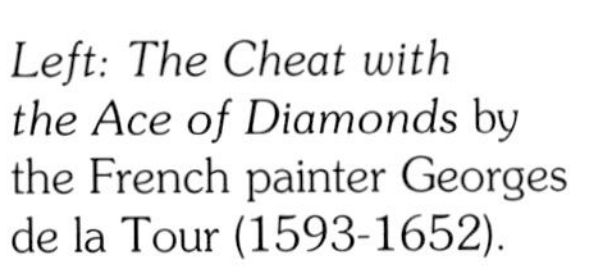

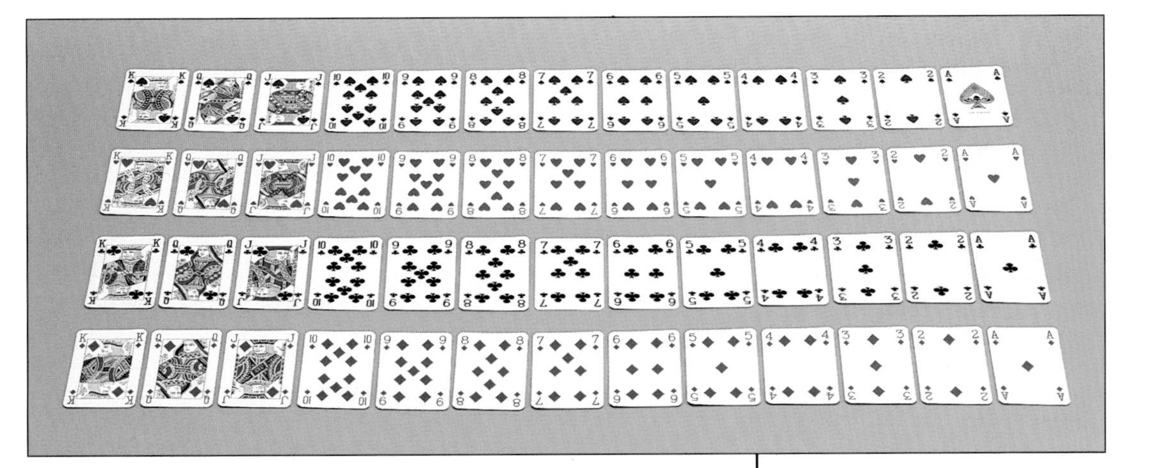

THE ORIGINS OF CARD GAMES

The majority of card games played in Britain initially came from France at various stages in history, for instance Napoleon, known in Britain as Nap, and *Vingt-et-Un* renamed Pontoon or Blackjack. A version of the French game *poque* (meaning "to bluff") found its way, with others, via emigrants to the United States of America and became better known as the gambling game of Poker. Another derivation of the name Poker could be the German word *"pochen",* also meaning "to bluff or boast". Many card games involve gambling for money or prizes; some are simply for the amusement and pleasure of the solo player or a group of players and some are used for the purposes of divination.

In most card games played in Britain and America, the deck comprises 52 cards divided into four suits. Each suit contains the cards one, or Ace,

through to ten and includes the court cards Jack, Queen and King. In various parts of Continental Europe, the number of cards in a deck differs slightly.

Card decks and their countries of origin

Deck	*Suits*	*Court cards*	*No of cards*
UK and USA	Diamonds, Clubs, Hearts and Spades	Jack, Queen, King	52
The Tarot	Clubs, Cups, Swords and Coins	Knave, Knight Queen and King	78
French	Trefoils, Hearts, Pikeheads and Tiles	Valet, Queen King	52
Italian	Staves, Cups, Swords and Coins	Page, Knight King	40
Spanish	Staves, Cups, Swords and Coins	Jack/Queen, Knight/King	52
German	Leaves, Shields, Acorns and Hawkbells	Unter, Ober, König	36

DIAMONDS

Diamonds, the first suit in the deck, symbolizes Spring and its element is Air. Diamonds are ambitious, energetic, outgoing cards with initiative and enthusiasm. Diamonds represent the intellect, and energy drives are expressed in a logical, clear-thinking way. Court cards represent fair-, red- or grey-haired people with blue eyes.

ACE OF DIAMONDS

Divinatory meaning: Symbolizing the first and the last, numbers one and thirteen, the Ace of Diamonds represents potential completion. Crystal-clear logic and strong powers of reasoning nurture ambitious, creative plans. Signifying hope and renewal, enthusiasm, energy and a single-minded will to win, there is some insensitivity to the feelings of others.
Reverse meaning: The will to win is there, but a lack of drive and motivation inhibits potential. Loss of direction. Set-backs and delays. Projects do not get off the ground.

KING OF DIAMONDS

Divinatory meaning: The King of Diamonds is a practical, disciplined character, a success in business and with women. An imposing figure commanding some respect, ambitious career plans tend to come first. Emotions are inhibited in this powerful, outgoing card.
Reverse meaning: A dogmatic, obstinate man. A devious schemer. Deceptions are revealed. Bitter dispute.

QUEEN OF DIAMONDS

Divinatory meaning: The Queen of Diamonds is a strong, physically attractive woman with a fertile imagination. She is positive and knows her own mind. Her status in life, achieved by endeavour and the will to succeed, is envied.
Reverse meaning: Injury caused by back-biting and malicious gossip. A spiteful woman. Hard-hearted authoritarian.

JACK OF DIAMONDS

Divinatory meaning: Generally representing a fair-haired youth, the Jack of Diamonds is charming, intelligent and keenly business-orientated. If this card symbolizes an adult, there is ambition with immaturity and lack of know-how inhibiting realization of full potential.
Reverse meaning: Unreliable and stubborn person unwilling to admit he is wrong. Misleading, and a troublemaker.

TEN

Divinatory meaning: The Ten of Diamonds signifies completion; a phase ends relating to intellectual and practical matters. Change involving journeys; money and career.
Reverse meaning: Threat of failure brings anxiety. Loss of direction. Pessimism.

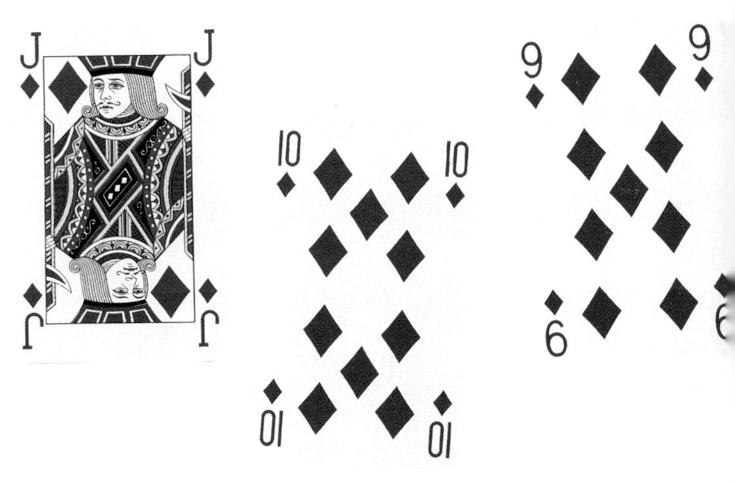

NINE

Divinatory meaning: The Nine of Diamonds indicates new interests ahead; promotion or a new business venture. Opportunities should be seized.
Reverse meaning: Delay. Dispute. Obstacles. Failure to embrace new ideas. Self-doubt dissipates energy.

EIGHT

Divinatory meaning: Signifying equality and negation, the Eight of Diamonds indicates an *impasse* in career and energy drives. Stimulation is required to progress further.
Reverse meaning: Indecision leads to lost opportunities. Loss of energy. Self-recrimination.

SEVEN

Divinatory meaning: The Seven of Diamonds indicates positive success. Vital energies combined with reason and logic bring self-confidence and material benefits.
Reverse meaning: Lack of vitality and drive. Reassess personal motives and attitudes.

SIX

Divinatory meaning: The Six of Diamonds indicates that goals are achieved when projects are carefully carried through. Caution is required when signing documents and discretion should be maintained.
Reverse meaning: Documents mislaid. Plans disrupted. Information leaked.

FIVE

Divinatory meaning: The Five of Diamonds, representing the personal ability to meet challenge, promises future success, if positive opportunities offered are taken.
Reverse meaning: Despondency due to lack of success. Inability to persevere.

FOUR

Divinatory meaning: The Four of Diamonds signifies that difficult decisions are to be made relating to practical issues: career, home or material possessions. Indecision leads to insecurity.
Reverse meaning: Instability. Hastily-made plans fail. Self-doubt.

THREE

Divinatory meaning: The Three of Diamonds indicates that soundly-based plans for the future can now be progressed with flair, energy and determination.
Reverse meaning: Hope and ambitions thwarted due to lack of drive.

TWO

Divinatory meaning: Business or domestic partnerships are highlighted by the Two of Diamonds. Ideals and experiences of both partners are needed to create a productive whole.
Reverse meaning: Incompatibility and opposition in practical partnership matters.

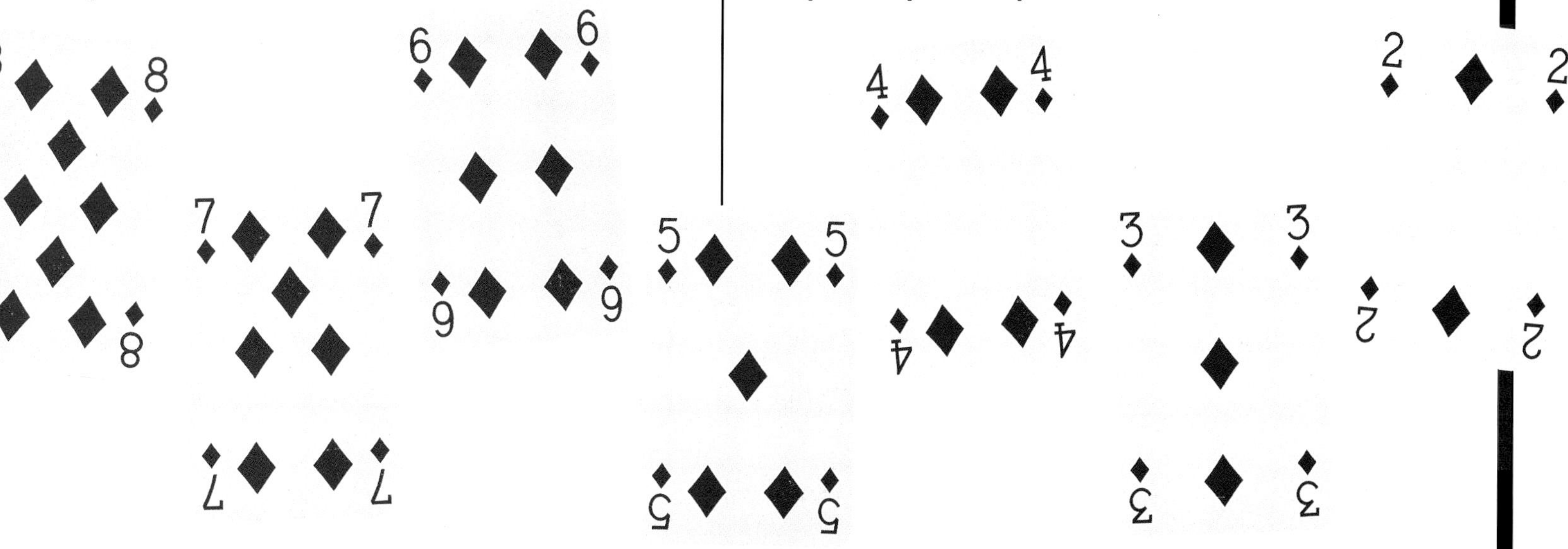

CLUBS

Clubs, the second suit in the deck, epitomizes Summer and its element is Fire. Full of determination and hope, Clubs indicate personal wealth and financial situations. Career relationships with money are also indicated and energy drives are expressed with fire and burning enthusiasm. Court cards represent brown- or dark-haired people with warm brown eyes.

ACE OF CLUBS

Divinatory meaning: The Ace of Clubs brings the potential for financial wealth and the necessary drive to realize that potential, or possible gifts and prizes of a substantial nature. Rewards may also be those of public recognition or of personal spiritual growth. There is a tendency to be "happy go lucky" and spiritual needs should not be relinquished in pursuit of physical gain.
Reverse meaning: Financial poverty. Total dependence on physical wealth. Rash money-raising schemes fail. Lack of rewarding inner contentment.

KING OF CLUBS

Divinatory meaning: The King of Clubs, a generous, honest man, accrues material riches with ease, and bold, imaginative schemes bring much personal wealth. Achievements admired, his advice is sought both in the personal and corporate financial fields.
Reverse meaning: Miserliness on physical and spiritual levels. Inability to accept change. Avarice turns away friends.

QUEEN OF CLUBS

Divinatory meaning: The Queen of Clubs is intelligent, resourceful and efficient; used to money and the luxuries it can buy. A warm, vital person, the envy of other women, this queen is self-centred and often marries for money.
Reverse meaning: A greedy, spiteful woman whose friends have deserted her. Inquisitiveness and prying habits annoy others.

JACK OF CLUBS

Divinatory meaning: The Jack of Clubs can represent an enterprising youth and budding tycoon with more ambition than academic prowess. Chances taken often hit the jackpot. When this card signifies an adult, there is decreased drive with plans remaining unrealized.
Reverse meaning: Hot-headed, misplaced drive creates restlessness and superficiality. Unreliability. Dishonesty.

TEN

Divinatory meaning: One cycle closes and the Ten of Clubs starts another with promise of a substantial sum of money, possibly from an unexpected source.
Reverse meaning: Spendthrift habits dissipate savings. Despondency. Loss of incentive.

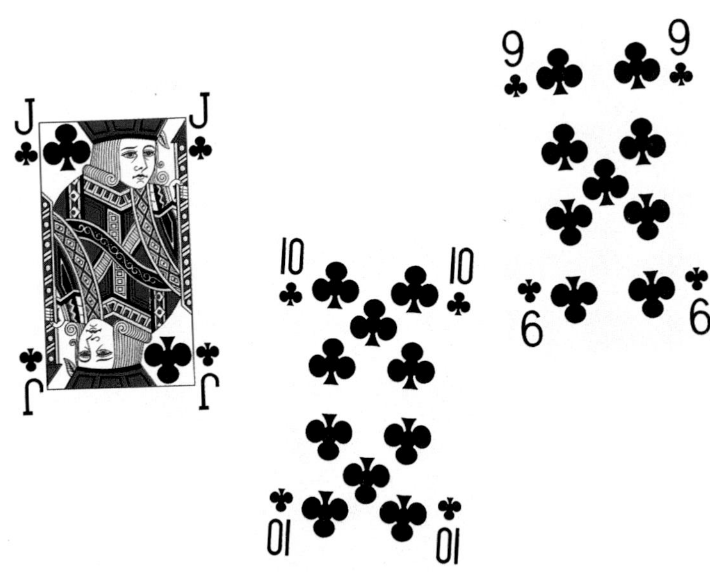

NINE

Divinatory meaning: The Nine of Clubs indicates an excellent financial outlook. Richness prevails in all areas; prosperous marriage or partnership; financial arrangements settled; security and happiness.
Reverse meaning: Imminent collapse of financial security. Control expenditure now.

EIGHT

Divinatory meaning: The Eight of Clubs suggests some anxiety regarding money. An element of risk makes money-making plans a gamble at this time.
Reverse meaning: Gambling instincts should be controlled. Better safe than sorry.

SEVEN

Divinatory meaning: Signifying personal success, the Seven of Clubs warns that money-making plans should be thoroughly checked. Increased business know-how and personal effort is encouraged.
Reverse meaning: Slipshod accounting leads to financial ruin.

SIX

Divinatory meaning: The Six of Clubs brings rewards for judicious, careful business planning and hard work. Pressure is unavoidable but business remains buoyant. Possible cash loan.
Reverse meaning: Happy-go-lucky attitude results in financial ruin.

FIVE

Divinatory meaning: The Five of Clubs brings hope for the future. Building on firm financial foundations, a new direction initiates substantial rewards. Partnership profits and inheritances are indicated.
Reverse meaning: Financial losses through doubtful speculation.

FOUR

Divinatory meaning: Stressing balance and harmony in business relationships, the Four of Clubs emphasizes care relating to personal possessions, i.e. the loss of jewellery, keys, purse or cash.
Reverse meaning: Difficulties, distrust and delays. Hasty moves will rebound.

THREE

Divinatory meaning: The Three of Clubs represents an energetic, creative trend bringing financial stability and material rewards. Businesses expand; personal fulfilment flourishes.
Reverse meaning: Self-recrimination follows wasted opportunities. Despair, but no effort made to improve.

TWO

Divinatory meaning: Combined finances or partnerships cause clashes. Opposition in joint ventures. The Two of Clubs warns against forming business partnerships at this time.
Reverse meaning: Opposition destroys initiative and drive. Spiteful partners cause problems.

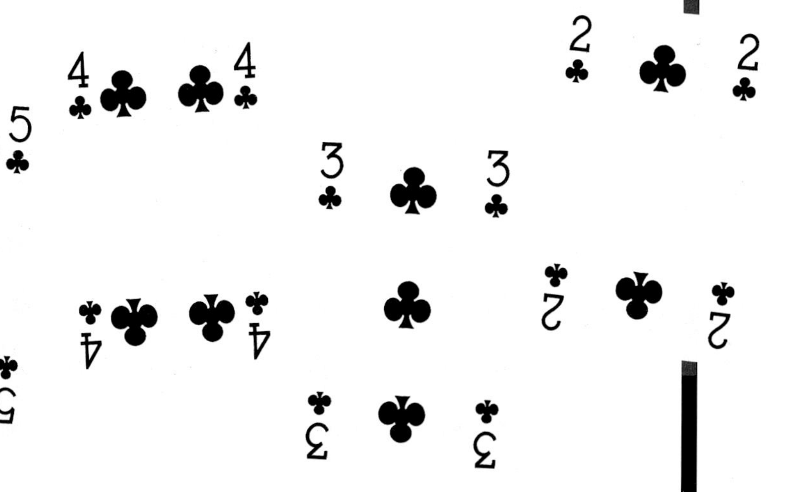

HEARTS

Hearts, the third suit in the deck, represents Autumn and its element is Water. Compassionate and emotional, Hearts symbolize a mellow maturity, home, family and warm maternal feelings. "Hearts are in the right place" and energy drives are expressed with sensitivity and emotion. Court cards represent fair- or white-haired people with blue or light-coloured eyes.

ACE OF HEARTS

Divinatory meaning: The Ace of Hearts contains all that the heart desires. There is love and compassion on all levels; warm family feelings; romantic love and kindliness shown to all living things. Signifying fertile beginnings, new and lasting friendships and relationships, happiness in the home and good news, there is a need to control emotions, exercise logic and not let "the heart rule the head".
Reverse meaning: Unsettled home life. Lack of feeling for others. Unkindness and emotional bleakness.

KING OF HEARTS

Divinatory meaning: The King of Hearts is a warm, compassionate and romantic person; he is home-loving and a generous father. Emotions triumph over reason and logic and when eventually sexual ardour declines, he will become withdrawn and often spiritually orientated.
Reverse meaning: Indiscretions. Rash judgement. Indulgence in sexual gratification does not bring fulfilment.

QUEEN OF HEARTS

Divinatory meaning: Representing the lovely young bride and the warm, desirable, faithful wife, the Queen of Hearts in maturity becomes the domesticated homebody whose horizons become increasingly limited. Sensitive, emotional and artistic, this queen probably has mediumistic capabilities.
Reverse meaning: Self-absorption and self-centredness makes a boring person. Daydreams overtake reality. Domestic disenchantment.

JACK OF HEARTS

Divinatory meaning: A happy young boy, the Jack of Hearts is a kind, friendly person but one who is immature and agelessly Peter Pan-like. A naive daydreamer, this Jack is a likeable lover but when bored or inactive can become depressed.
Reverse meaning: Short-tempered. Can wallow permanently in self-pity if rejected in love.

TEN

Divinatory meaning: A new phase begins. Heartfelt happiness and joy is promised by the Ten of Hearts. Good news concerning family. The birth of a baby?
Reverse meaning: Tension. Family arguments. Romantic opportunities wasted.

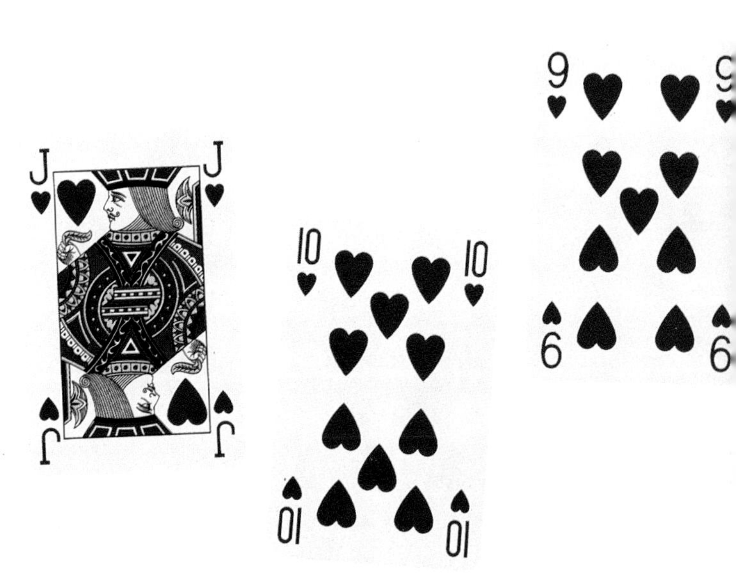

NINE

Divinatory meaning: The Nine of Hearts grants heart's desires. Secret dreams come true. Wishes fulfilled relating to all areas of life, especially family.
Reverse meaning: Lovers' ardour is over-enthusiastic. Intentions are misunderstood.

EIGHT

Divinatory meaning: In romantic affairs, the Eight of Hearts can bring joy or disappointment. It's make-or-break time; feelings are sensitive; hasty actions regretted.
Reverse meaning: Obstacles in romantic relationships. Opposition. Prejudice.

SEVEN

Divinatory meaning: The Seven of Hearts holds great potential for personal happiness, if there is emotional balance and harmony. Romantic dreams come true; wisdom and inner peace follows.
Reverse meaning: Selfishness. Disappointment in love.

SIX

Divinatory meaning: Heart's desires lie ahead. The Six of Hearts indicates that all is possible, at a price. Acceptable compromise, self-sacrifice and effort are called for.
Reverse meaning: Frustration. Self-imposed sacrifice drains energies.

FIVE

Divinatory meaning: Romantic relationships require cautious handling warns the Five of Hearts. Impassioned outbursts lead to misunderstanding. Short-sighted policies followed at the expense of reason.
Reverse meaning: Apathy and laziness lead to opportunities missed.

FOUR

Divinatory meaning: The Four of Hearts indicates an uneasy state of affairs in family or romantic relationships. Careful consideration is required before any action is taken.
Reverse meaning: Unjust dealings in emotional affairs. Remorse. Regret.

THREE

Divinatory meaning: Heartfelt emotions bring their reward promises the Three of Hearts. Relationships flourish in a fertile, creative way. News of a birth or an imaginative project?
Reverse meaning: Energies and emotions exhausted. Judgement impaired.

TWO

Divinatory meaning: Two hearts merge as one; satisfying romantic and marriage partnerships flourish vows the Two of Hearts. The ultimate balance and harmony of Two.
Reverse meaning: Disharmony and instability relating to emotional relationships.

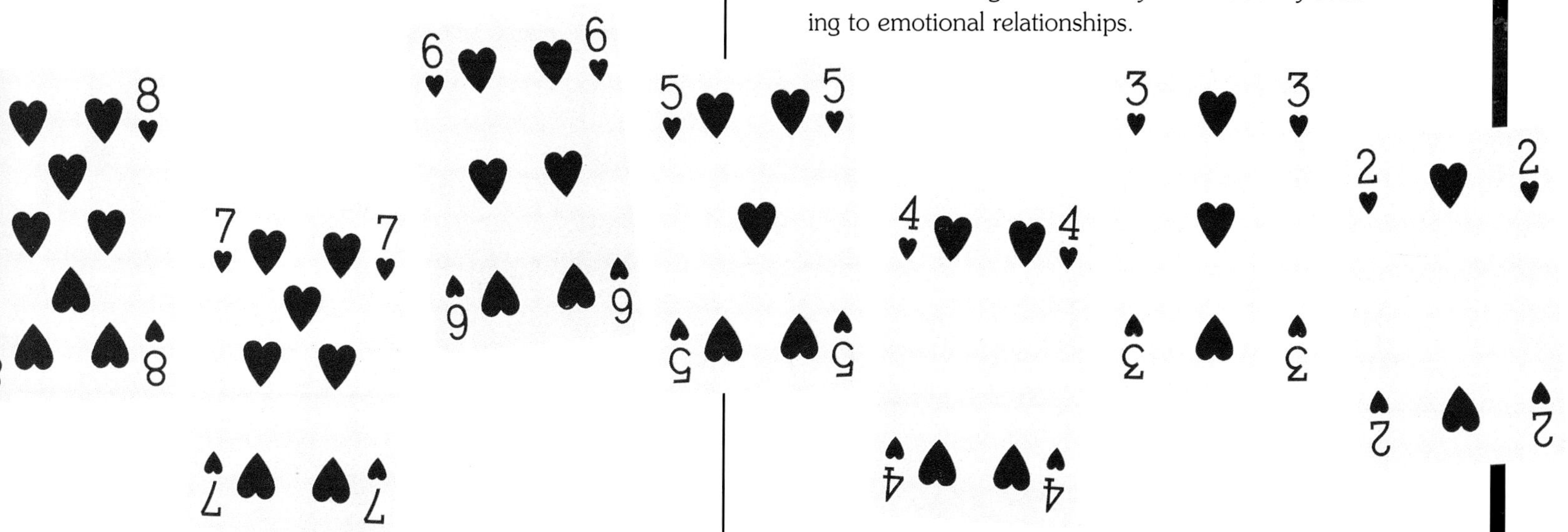

SPADES

Spades, the fourth suit in the deck, symbolizes Winter and its element is Earth. Spades recall the dark bleakness of sleeping earth; old age and sadness. Difficulties and obstacles prevail and all is expressed with authoritarianism, caution and coldness. Court cards represent dark- or black-haired people with dark eyes.

ACE OF SPADES

Divinatory meaning: Like the Tarot's Death (XIII) card, the Ace of Spades indicates the death of one phase prior to the rebirth of a new one. Cataclysmic happenings relating to all areas of life will erupt, bringing matters to a head. Caution on all fronts is required – beware of dangers ahead. Expressed in an eruptive, Plutonic way, the Ace of Spades paves the way for new beginnings.
Reverse meaning: Disharmony with partners and family. Instability in emotional relationships. Bad news. Personal feelings revealed endanger relationships.

KING OF SPADES

Divinatory meaning: Dynamic and authoritarian, the King of Spades is ruled by intellect, relentlessly ignoring instincts and intuition. Critical of others and showing formidable ruthlessness to achieve his ends, this powerful King is often drawn to government, politics or the law.
Reverse meaning: Unscrupulous dealings lead to loneliness. Barriers and obstacles cause disruption and chaos.

QUEEN OF SPADES

Divinatory meaning: Unscrupulous woman, sly and cunning; ruthless and hard-hearted, the Queen of Spades is a law unto herself. She is dangerous in the extreme and plots the downfall of others. Beware. Never underestimate this woman.
Reverse meaning: A crafty, spiteful woman who may attack verbally or otherwise. Bleakness and desolation.

JACK OF SPADES

Divinatory meaning: Representing a young boy, the Jack of Spades is seen as a miscreant, but generally it symbolizes an emotionally immature adult man. Harbouring outlandish delusions of self-importance, this is an inadequate person. Leadership qualities, if any, will descend into despotism.
Reverse meaning: An untrustworthy, treacherous male person. Inability to admit inadequacies and mistakes.

TEN

Divinatory meaning: The Ten of Spades indicates the end of a difficult phase which brought severe challenge in all areas. Personal bitterness, frustration, failure and desolation.
Reverse meaning: Matters deteriorate further. Recurring problems.

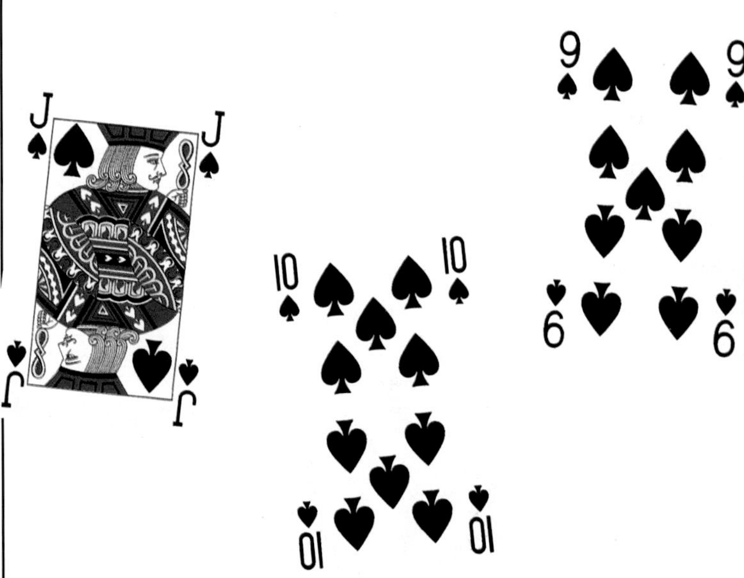

NINE

Divinatory meaning: Affecting other suits around it, the negative Nine of Spades drains energies and tests the physical and mental resources. Illnesses revealed; inner tensions build up.
Reverse meaning: Health problems. Poverty. Rejection. Depression.

EIGHT

Divinatory meaning: An unfortunate card, the Eight of Spades creates obstacles, disruptions, disputes and dilemmas. Arguments and clashes are evenly matched. Nothing is resolved. Deadlock.
Reverse meaning: Persistent misfortune. Efforts come to nothing. Despondency.

SEVEN

Divinatory meaning: The Seven of Spades reveals secret fears and inner doubts. Gloom and despondency haunt every occasion. An unwillingness to accept life philosophically.
Reverse meaning: Negativity persists. Malicious, vengeful thoughts are harboured.

SIX

Divinatory meaning: Set-backs and disappointments are the message of the Six of Spades. Little reward for sustained effort. Minor problems and doubts cause delays and obstacles.
Reverse meaning: Ongoing minor disasters. No improvement.

FIVE

Divinatory meaning: Miscalculations and misunderstandings cause discouraging trends in most areas warns the Five of Spades. But with determined effort, the outcome could improve.
Reverse meaning: Unexpected set-backs. Avoid legal conflict.

FOUR

Divinatory meaning: The negative Four of Spades indicates frustrating deadlocks. Domestic, romantic and financial aspects are all affected. Nothing will improve matters at the present time.
Reverse meaning: Cowardice and delaying tactics compound troubles.

THREE

Divinatory meaning: Interference by a third party or unfortunate circumstance threatens financial or emotional stability warns the Three of Spades. Beware of third business partners; a disruptive child or troublesome adult.
Reverse meaning: Disharmony. Broken agreements. Pessimistic outlook.

TWO

Divinatory meaning: Opposition and a parting of the ways. Pessimism is experienced, also optimism for a hopeful outcome. A bleak Winter of discontent followed by the promise of Spring is symbolized by the Two of Spades.
Reverse meaning: Despair is alleviated by hope.

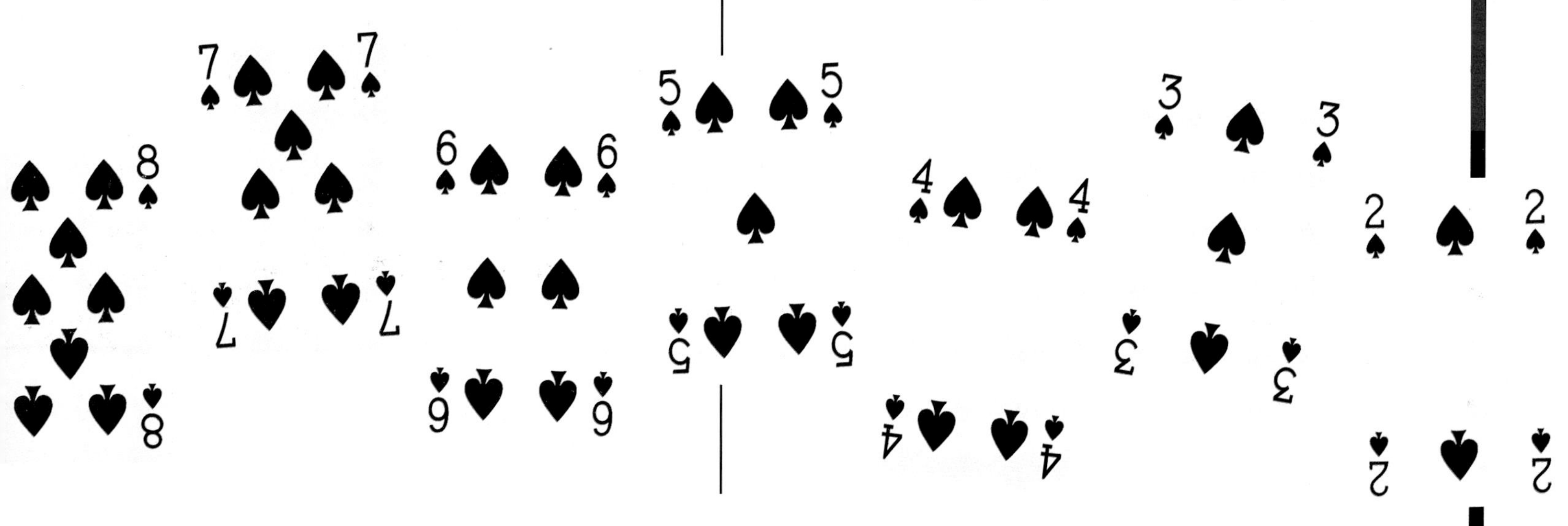

THE JOKER

The counterpart of The Fool in the Major Arcana of the Tarot, the Joker in cartomancy – symbolizing sense and nonsense, wisdom and folly – is also unnumbered and can represent all and nothing. As an extra card, the Joker may be placed, or appear, anywhere in the deck. In this way it is described as "wild" and in some card games can rank above any other card.

PLAYING THE CLOWN

In medieval times, every court had its jester, or joker, whose function it was to bring laughter to the King, Queen and their courtiers by performing acts of buffoonery. The jester was perhaps not so foolish as he looked in his gaily coloured costume, clowning around in pointed shoes with hat, stick and jingling bells. It is said that it takes a wise man to criticize his master, albeit in jest, and get away with it. The jester did just that, with dexterity, wit and an innocent, guileless charm!

Symbolizing the unknown potential within us all, the Joker, when it appears in a reading, brings with it the element of surprise accompanied by surges of vital energy. Often with a flash of inspirational brilliance, transformations take place; situations about face; new doors are opened and new directions indicated. An enthusiastic, enquiring and carefree character, the Joker is an adept juggler as he plays fool and wise man at the same time. When he leaps onto the scene, prepare to expect the unexpected! Should the Joker suddenly appear in a spread, do not be tempted to remove it or replace it with another card. The Joker has jumped in with a special message which must be heeded.

THE JOKER'S JOURNEY

Divinatory meaning: Representing potential unfulfilled and, like The Fool, seeking enlightenment as he progresses along the path of life, the Joker journeys through the deck, confronting the suits, their numbers and the varying individual forces of the cards, and is influenced by these accordingly. The Joker's presence in a reading can be volatile; its effect enlightening and changeful. Emotional situations are given a profound shaking-up and whether the outcome is welcome or not, at least new aspects are examined with illuminating clarity.

In financial and business affairs, energy drives and inspired know-how promise excellent results. Rewards and awards are the outcome for creative and intellectual effort and transformations occur, as it were, overnight. Tense and cautious attitudes disappear, making way for a new, relaxed approach to life in general.

Reverse meaning: The fool in the Joker triumphs. Carelessness and a devious cunning prevail. The single-minded pursuit of pleasure threatens financial and emotional stability. General status is diminished.

Left: The philosophical Fool observes life at all levels . . .

Left: Allegorical works of art often include The Jester. *The Parable of the Prodigal Son* is no exception.

COMBINATIONS OF CARDS

Combinations of cards and their position in relation to other cards in a spread holds considerable significance and can bring added depth to a reading. Listed below are a variety of combinations which may be encountered when reading a spread of cards.

COMBINATIONS AND THEIR MEANINGS

Two Aces: Marriage. An affair. Union.
Three Aces: Harmony. Fertility. Birth.
Four Aces: Success. Celebration. Joy.

Two Kings: Stable partnership. Good advice.
Three Kings: Good fortune and firm friends.
Four Kings: Honourable success. Victory.

Two Queens: A firm friendship but beware of gossip.
Three Queens: Malicious gossip.
Four Queens: Scandal and treachery.

Two Jacks: Bickering. Heated discussion and debate
Three Jacks: Disharmony in the family.
Four Jacks: Disruptions. Rifts lead to new alliances.

Two Tens: Change in home, career or environment.
Three Tens: Financial problems. Litigation. Repayments.
Four Tens: Good fortune in business matters.

Two Nines: Minor change professionally may bring financial gain.
Three Nines: Successful enterprise.
Four Nines: Pleasant surprise.

Two Eights: Partnership disputes.
Three Eights: Minor anxieties.
Four Eights: Anxiety. Frustration. Deadlock.

Two Sevens: Romantic love fulfilled.
Three Sevens: New project or birth of a child.
Four Sevens: Balance. Harmony. Equilibrium.

Two Sixes: Arguments. Confrontation.
Three Sixes Efforts rewarded.
Four Sixes: Goals achieved but obstacles may follow.

Two Fives: Partners are at odds.
Three Fives: Difficulties surmounted.
Four Fives: Sound foundations but difficulties lie ahead.

Two Fours Partnership deadlock. Stalemate.
Three Fours: Inspiration brings rewards.
Four Fours: Equality. Stability but going nowhere.

Two Threes: Options open. Outlook promising.
Three Threes: Success and good fortune come easily.

Four Threes: Happiness and good fortune but beware of complacency.

Two Twos: Partners separate.
Three Twos: Partnerships flourish.
Four Twos: Relationships end. A new one awaits.

The Joker: Prepare for the unexpected. Anything might happen!

Ace of Diamonds among several Clubs: Quick thinking benefits personal finances.

Ace of Diamonds among several Hearts: Business project delayed because of emotional problems.

Ace of Diamonds among several Spades: Ambitious project encounters obstacles.

Ace of Clubs among several Diamonds: Increase in wealth and status.

Ace of Clubs among several Hearts: Financial gains bring heartfelt joy.

Ace of Clubs among several Spades: Loss of personal wealth.

Ace of Hearts among several Diamonds: Romance at work or encountered on a journey.

Ace of Hearts among several Clubs: Heartfelt generosity.

Ace of Hearts among several Spades: An affair of the heart suffers serious setbacks.

Ace of Spades among several Diamonds: Ambitious plans unexpectedly curtailed.

Ace of Spades among several Hearts: Emotional matters take a turn for the worse.

Ace of Spades among several Clubs: Financial matters come to a head.

A Jack next to a King or Queen: News for good or ill is passed on, depending on the Jack's suit, i.e. Diamonds: Malicious gossip; Clubs: Good tidings; Hearts: News of a romance; Spades: Bad tidings.

The Queen of Spades between a King and another Queen: An unscrupulous woman stands between husband and wife.

A number of mixed court cards: A happy, festive occasion.

Mainly red cards in the spread: Predominantly concerned with women and/or feminine activities.

Mainly black cards in the spread: Predominantly concerned with men and/or masculine activities.

COURT CARDS

Court cards may be used as client cards or significators in a reading. Two groups are outlined below and represent two different angles from which court cards can be viewed. The first group denotes physical and personality aspects of the cards in the four suits and the second outlines external characteristics and likely fields of endeavour.

According to the nature of the Enquirer's query, the Reader will select a card from the appropriate category. For a man, a King is chosen; for a woman or young girl, a Queen is chosen and for a young boy, a Jack is chosen. In some instances, the Jack may also represent a youthful-looking adult male.

FOR A GENERAL OR PERSONAL RELATIONSHIP READING

Diamond court cards: Representing fair-, red- or grey-haired people with pale complexions and blue eyes. Diamonds are generally slim, sophisticated and elegant with witty, charming personalities.

Heart court cards: Fair- or white-haired people with warmly coloured complexions and blue or light-coloured eyes. Hearts are generally plump with warm and friendly personalities.

Club court cards: Brown- or dark-haired people with rich, colourful complexions and warm brown eyes. Clubs are generally lively, energetic people with warm, generous natures.

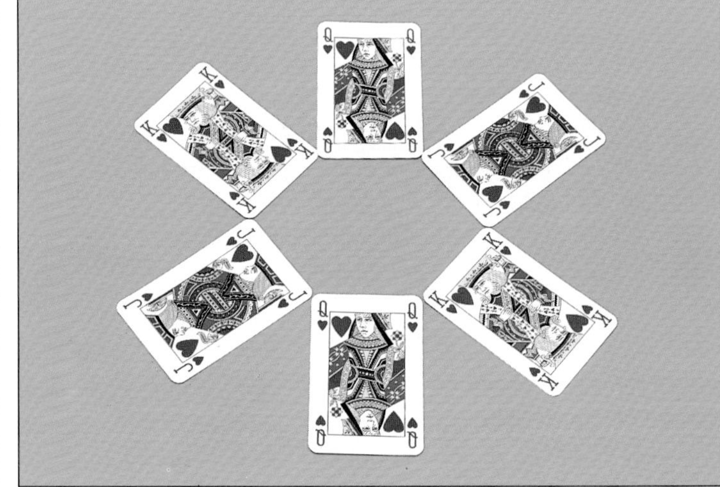

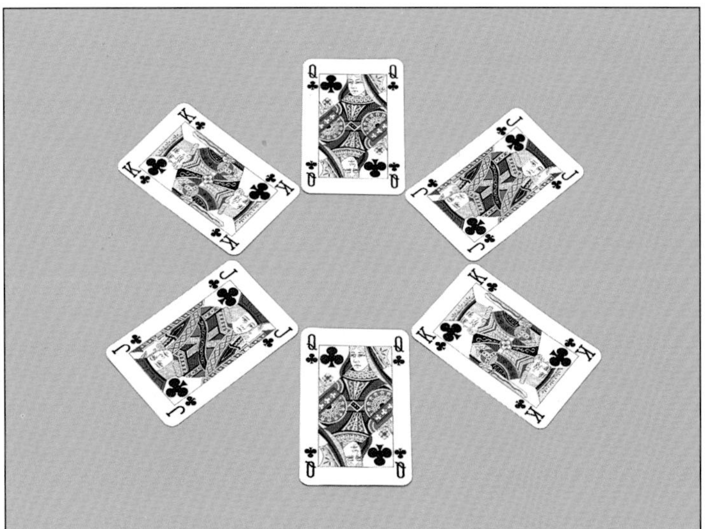

Spade court cards: Dark- or black-haired people with sallow complexions and dark eyes. Spades are powerful, compelling people with an abundance of physical energy and dynamism.

FOR MORE SPECIALIZED READINGS

Diamond court cards: Representing the intellect, with particular emphasis on work involving the capacity for thinking. Efficient, enthusiastic, ambitious and initiatory, careers can be in the professional fields: communications, writing, broadcasting, the travel industry and all practical matters relating to business.

Heart court cards: Representing those closely involved with emotional problems; matters of the heart; romantic relationships, heartfelt links with home and family. Careers can be in the caring professions: nurse, doctor, priest, social worker, teacher, child-minder.

Club court cards: Representing those with financial interests, in both the personal and commercial sectors. Excelling in investment and business deals and often they relate to business tycoons. Careers can be in banking, stocks and shares, corporate finance or insurance broking.

Spade court cards: Representing those who are in the depths of despair and without physical or emotional security. Health problems and negativity in all areas surround the Spade. Careers can be in authoritarian fields: judges, lawyers, the armed forces, politicians and all those in high office.

COURT CARD RELATIONSHIPS

Special attention should be paid to the court cards in a spread since these represent the people and personal relationships in the Enquirer's life. Look at the overall picture of the lay-out and see which suits most of the court cards are in.

An important point to remember is that if the client card and the court cards are all (or almost all) of the same suit, there will be a strong and positive link between the cards and the Enquirer.

Court cards which are "opposite" from the client card are also important. Diamonds are opposite Hearts, and Clubs are opposite Spades. These "opposites" hold a negative connection or relationship. For example, the Queen of Clubs and the King of Clubs may well enjoy a strong, generous and wealthy relationship, whereas a linking of the Queen of Clubs and the King of Spades would, more than likely, end in grief and misery. (The meanings of the suits and their court cards are summarized on pp 72-79.)

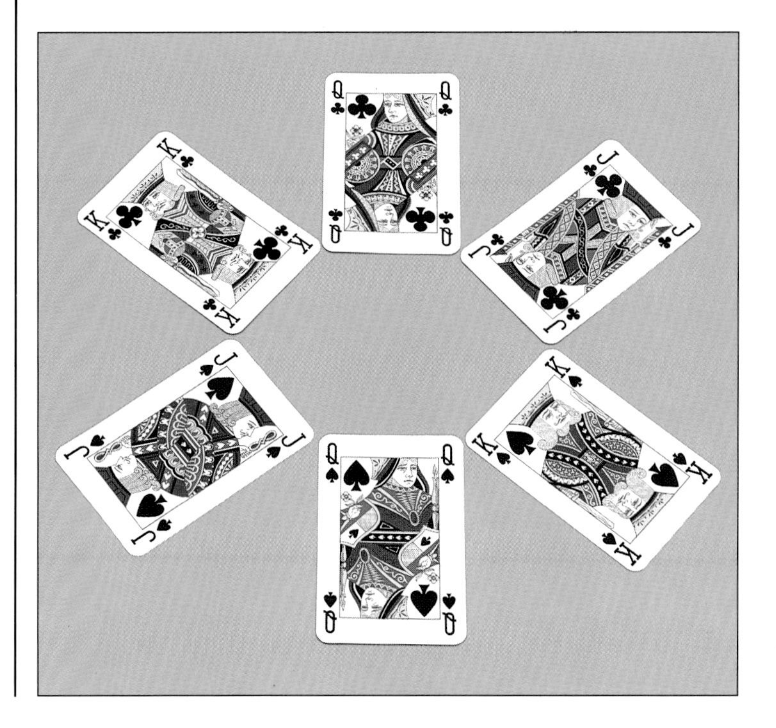

CLIENT CARDS AND THEIR USAGE

Most Readers devise their own particular ritual when selecting a client card or significator. Methods can differ, however, depending on the nature of the spreads used. For specialized readings, the client card is selected by the Reader. In spreads which rely on the personal vibrations of the Enquirer being absorbed into a spread, he or she can select a card from a fan proffered by the Reader. The Enquirer will then carefully replace the card in the fan, its value unseen by them but revealed to the Reader. The Enquirer may also cut the deck, once to the left with the left hand (**1**). The card at the top of pile two will be the client card (**2**,**3**).

1

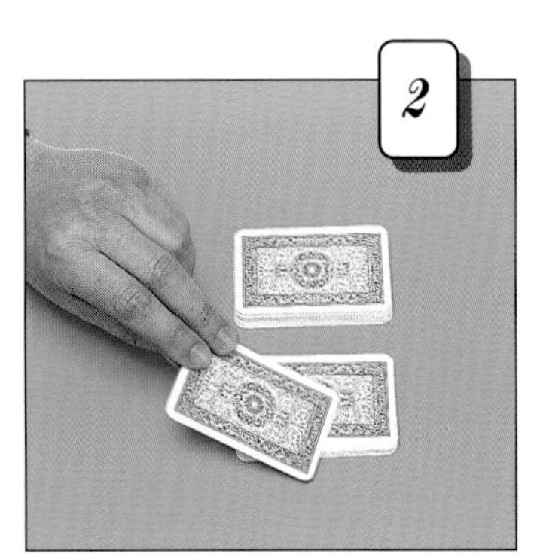

2

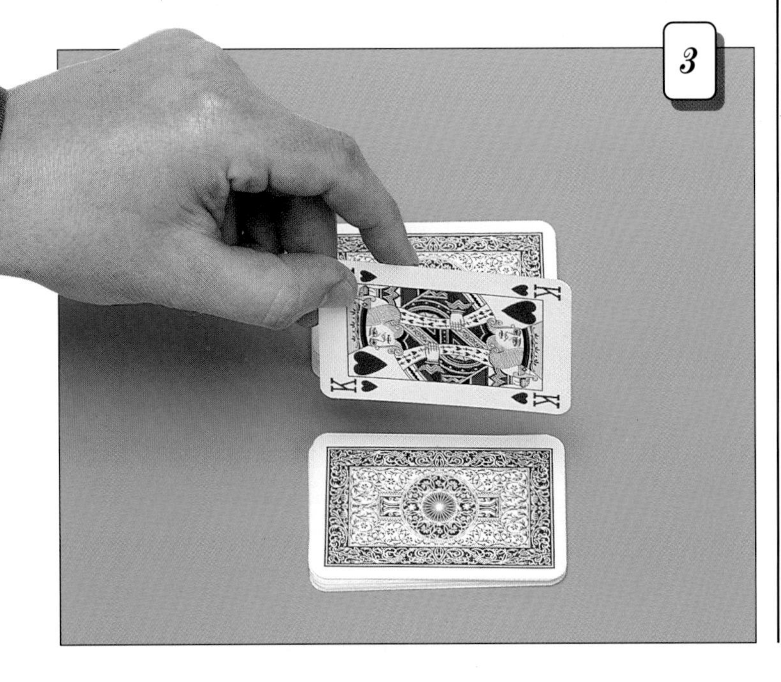

3

WILL THE CARD APPEAR?

Following the selection of the client card, the Reader (who has noted its identity) may return it to the deck. As appropriate, the Reader or the Enquirer will then shuffle the cards. If the client card does not appear in the first lay-out, shuffle and try again. This procedure may be followed three times. If the client card still does not appear, proceed with the lay-out without it, since it is obvious that this card wishes to remain silent!

THE CLIENT CARD AND THE COURT CARDS IN ACTION

We have seen how the Reader may select a court card as the client card, or significator, in relation to the Enquirer's question. The close link that the client card has with the Enquirer has also been stressed. An example of that powerful connection is outlined below and right in a basic 5-card personal relationship spread. The closely interwoven meanings of the court cards, representing those who are close to the Enquirer, and the client card gives an insight into the immediate fortunes of the Enquirer.

Separate all the court cards in the deck; select the appropriate client card and place it on the table. Shuffle the remaining cards and starting from left to right, place two court cards on either side of the client card, giving five cards in all (**4**-**7**).

4

THE INTERPRETATION

The Enquirer, represented by the King of Hearts (**8**), is Stephen, a light-haired man with blue eyes and a warm, pleasant disposition. He is soon to be the centre of a highly charged emotional situation. It would appear that Stephen has a dark-haired lady friend – a lively, intelligent female who has her sights set on his heart – and his bank balance! This young woman will introduce another woman to Stephen, one who is destined to come between them in their relationship.

Stephen (King of Hearts) is destined to fall in no uncertain way for the lovely, fair-haired newcomer who, like himself, is warm, compassionate and home-loving (Queen of Hearts). Stephen and his new-found love get along famously, leaving the discarded lover (Queen of Clubs) to simmer on the sideline.

The situation is due to be resolved when an enterprising young male friend of Stephen's (Jack of Clubs) introduces to the scene a fair-haired young man, a kindly, romantic youth (Jack of Hearts), all set to captivate the resourceful Miss Clubs who sees in him much of what was in her former lover: warmth, generosity and romance. There is romance a-plenty in young Jack of Hearts and the lively Miss Clubs will probably keep him occupied – until a wealthier prospect comes along.

DIVINATION AND PSYCHIC POWER

Divination by means of cartomancy is equally as powerful psychically as is divination of the Tarot. Though seen merely as "ordinary playing cards" which are often used to "amuse oneself" as Ettiela playfully suggested, the 52-card deck of playing cards is one of the oldest tools for divination in history. Associated with the wandering bands of gypsies of long ago who passed through the Mediterranean areas foretelling the future, playing cards were seen as sacred objects, extensions of the various cultures and religions, anciently originating in Egypt with the Book of Thoth. As one of the oldest surviving reminders of man's unquenchable desire to read his fate, the cards are worthy of great respect.

HAVE RESPECT FOR THE CARDS

Representing ancient wisdoms beyond our normal understanding, it is appropriate that you treat your cards accordingly. Unless, in the course of a reading, an Enquirer is asked to do so, allow no-one to handle your cards. This, as with the ancient Tarot, precludes the aura of others from infiltrating or "fogging" the deck.

The psychic intuition will flow more easily when the diverse meanings of the cards become familiar to you. Handle your cards frequently so that they become part of you and your everyday life (**1**). Keep them in their own special resting place when not in use (**2**). Ritual, such as the method of selecting a significator or laying a spread, *must* flow and work for *you*. Dispense with elaborate rituals, unless they work for you, since these can stand in the way of your intuition, that early sixth sense, the

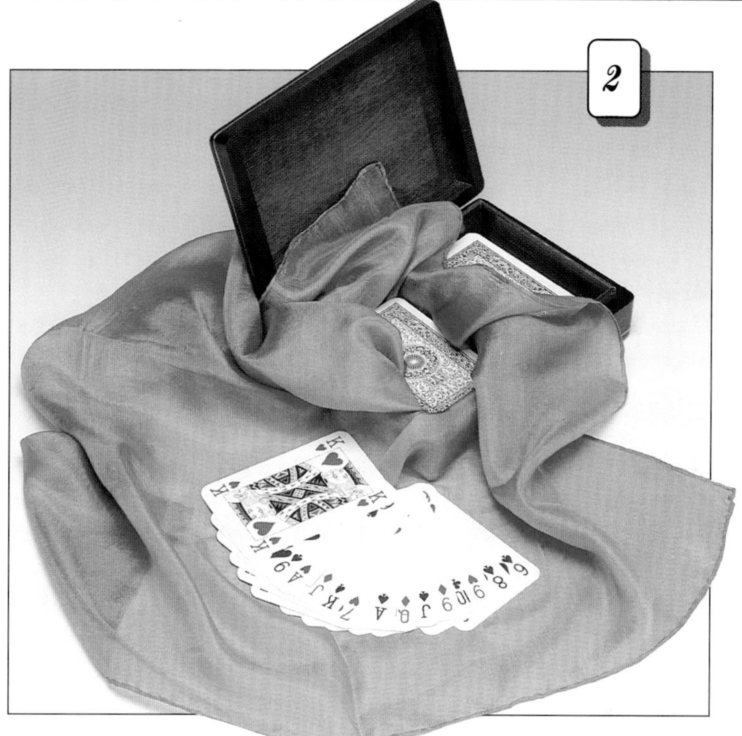

voice within that speaks to us before the intervention of conscious thought . . .

The message of the cards is interpreted through the Reader, whose personal powers of interpretation may well differ from those of another. In this way, readings, while basically bringing the same message, will differ according to each Reader's interpretation.

Experience and practice are the keywords and the more frequently the cards are used for the purpose of divination, the more confidence will grow. Increasingly, insight and intuition will bring an awareness of the possibilities which lie ahead in each fortune.

The psychologist Carl Gustav Jung spoke of "synchronicity", the psychic link existing between man and his environment. From the position of the planets at our birth and our corresponding personalities, to divination in all forms, plus synchronicity, defined as "meaningful coincidence", the cosmic relationship is present throughout. From ancient times Diviners have interpreted the underlying link existing between the Universe and ourselves. The saying "As above, so it is below" is attributed to the Ionian philosopher Anaximenes (c550B.C.), and this theory is encountered not only in astrology but also in the Tarot, cartomancy and other forms of divination. What is represented above is also reflected below in our everyday lives . . .

Left: The wisdom of Romany folk is well-known. This painting is *The Fortune Tellers* by Edward Charles Barnes (1856-82).

Right: When not in use, place your cards in their own "home" – a special box is ideal.

PRELIMINARIES

The table used for a reading may be square or round in shape; a card table is ideal but do make sure that it is large enough to allow freedom of movement and to avoid crowding the cards. A firm felt or baize covering is a good idea to prevent the cards from slipping. Subdued lighting or a low light dropped from the ceiling shining directly onto the cards will create a conducive atmosphere and give a special focus on the cards – after all, *they* are the star turn! Your own face and that of the Enquirer will be in shadow. Your deck should be used specifically for divination purposes and to maintain credibility, a good knowledge of the cards is essential. If there is doubt in your mind about the significance of the cards, a few notes placed discreetly below table-top level will assist.

PERSONAL RITUAL

Before beginning the reading, try consciously to centre yourself so that you are in the right frame of mind. Extricate your consciousness from external influences and relax. Taking your time, breathe slowly and deeply three times and allow your intuitive instincts to take over.

Hold the deck between your palms (**1**); sense its strength and feel its power. When you are ready, begin to shuffle the cards (**2**) using your own particular method – the one that feels right for you. Encourage the Enquirer to ask their question and, as you shuffle, the cards will absorb the personal vibrations of the Enquirer, and you will instinctively know which spread would be most appropriate for the question. You should now feel the positive energy of the cards and again, instinctively, know when to cease shuffling.

THE READING

According to the spread involved, select a client card or, alternatively, ask the Enquirer to select one as shown on page 86. The nature of their query should be uppermost in their minds as they do this. If appropriate, invite the Enquirer to shuffle the cards to impart his or her aura onto the deck, offering a closer involvement with their own destiny . . .

Maintaining your own psychic link with the cards, proceed to lay out the spread in a traditional form, or in your own particular way, as seems appropriate. The reading follows.

When the reading is completed, the cards are gathered together and thoroughly shuffled to remove present vibrations and to dissociate them from the last Enquirer. If another reading does not immediately follow, place your cards in their special resting place to await the next reading.

GENERAL TIPS

- To obtain the 32-card deck, which is generally preferred for divinatory purposes, discard the twos, threes, fours, fives and sixes of each suit.
- Three separate supplementary questions may be asked by the Enquirer during a reading, relating to the main query.
- How to incorporate a Cosmic Cut reading. Cut the deck with the left hand to produce two piles.

Take a card from the top of pile one and a card from the bottom of pile two. Set these aside for a "final word" on the main reading.

- The left hand is generally used to cut the cards since this hand is closest to the heart in both the physical and the emotional sense.
- For easier recognition of cards which are reversed, you may mark one end of the cards in the deck with a small pencil dot (**3**).
- Remember that the nine of Hearts is known as the Heart's Desire card. If this appears in the spread, it augurs well for the entire reading, lessening a bad fortune, confirming a good one!

TWO SINGLE-QUESTION METHODS

Single-question spreads are simple but nonetheless time-honoured methods of answering a single, direct question. The message and interpretation are limited but to the point. Additional queries stemming from the original question may be asked, but it is said that the cards begin to weary after two supplementary questions.

YES AND NO

Sample question (1): *"I am about to attend an interview for a new job. Will I be successful?"*

Invite the Enquirer to shuffle the 32-card deck until he or she feels ready to stop (**1**). With the left hand, the Enquirer then cuts the cards twice to the left, producing three piles (**2**). You, the Reader, turn up the last or bottom card of each pile (**3**). If all the cards are black, the answer to the question is a positive "No". If two are black and one is red, this means a less emphatic "No". Should the bottom card from each of the three piles be red, "Yes" is the answer, but this is affirmed with a degree of reservation if two cards are red and one is black (**4**).

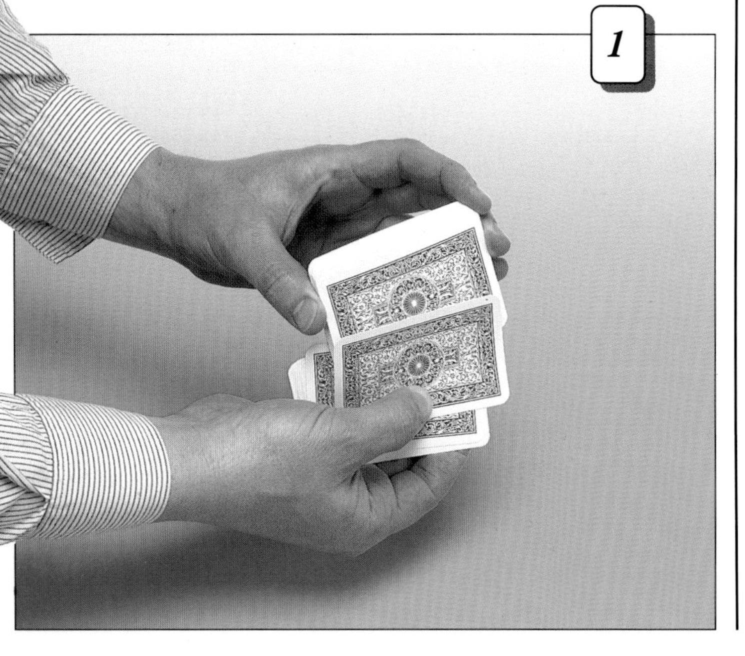

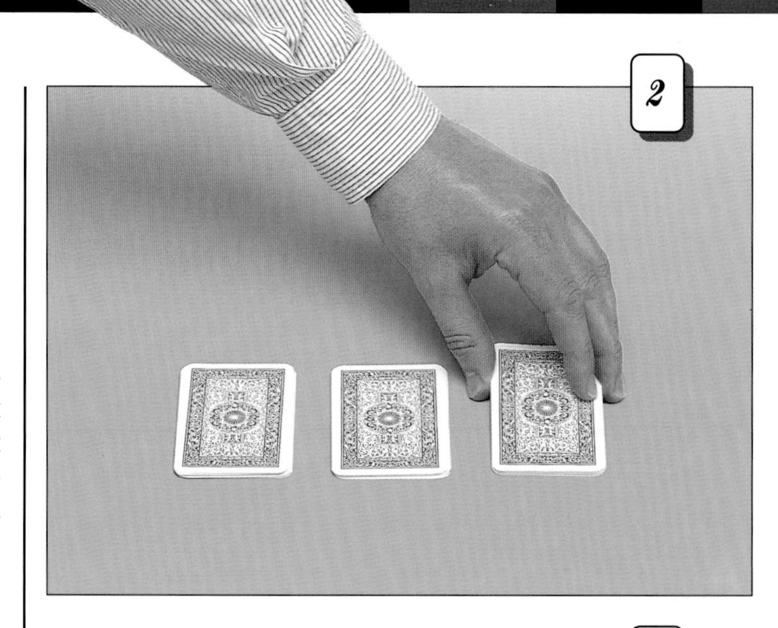

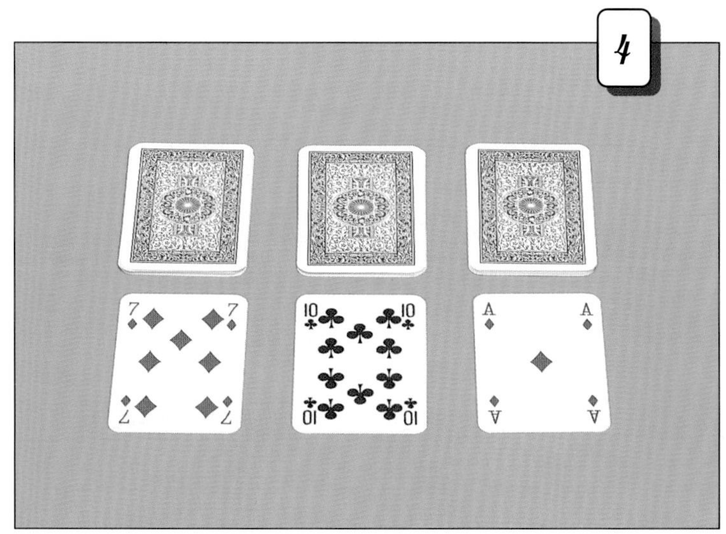

THREE OF SEVEN

Sample question (2): *"What of my immediate future?"*
The Enquirer shuffles the 32-card deck plus the Joker and with the left hand, cuts it to the left, placing the second pile on top of the first. The Reader lays out seven cards from the top of the deck, face down, in a row from the left (**5**). She turns up the first, fourth and seventh cards, and these are then read (**6**).

The seven cards represent the completion of a cycle and examination of cards one, four and seven gives a brief insight into the Enquirer's immediate past and future. Cards two and three indicate the past; cards five and six, the future. If black cards lie on the left side of the spread, this indicates an unfavourable past, and if on the right, an unfavourable future. If the two left-hand cards are red, the past has been favourable and if they lie to the right, the future looks optimistic. A mix of black and red cards will moderate the situation accordingly.

THE INTERPRETATION

Unexpected events in a romantic affair recently opened the eyes of the Enquirer, causing him to view his partner in a totally different light (Card One: Red Joker). Events were favourable enough at that time but accompanied by minor worries, probably regarding the relationship (Cards One and Two). A warm, compassionate man, however, the Enquirer (King of Hearts) considers placing the relationship on a permanent basis. There is personal happiness followed by minor anxieties, possibly career-related (Cards Five and Six). Energy drives will flourish and a single-minded will to win will further future ambitions (Card Seven: Ace of Diamonds).

5

6

THE FAN

The Fan is a classic spread which is eminently suitable for a deeply personal problem. The first thirteen cards include three client cards which represent the Enquirer and two other people significant in his or her current life. The remaining ten cards in the upper section of the spread indicate the general overall trend of present events. The final five cards lying beneath this section predict what the future holds for the Enquirer.

THE FAN

The Reader shuffles the 32-card deck and spreads it out, face down on the table. The Enquirer is invited to select eighteen cards, which is done using the left hand. Each card is given to the Reader who accepts them with the right hand (**1**) and places them in strict sequential order, in a pile (**2**). These cards are

1

2

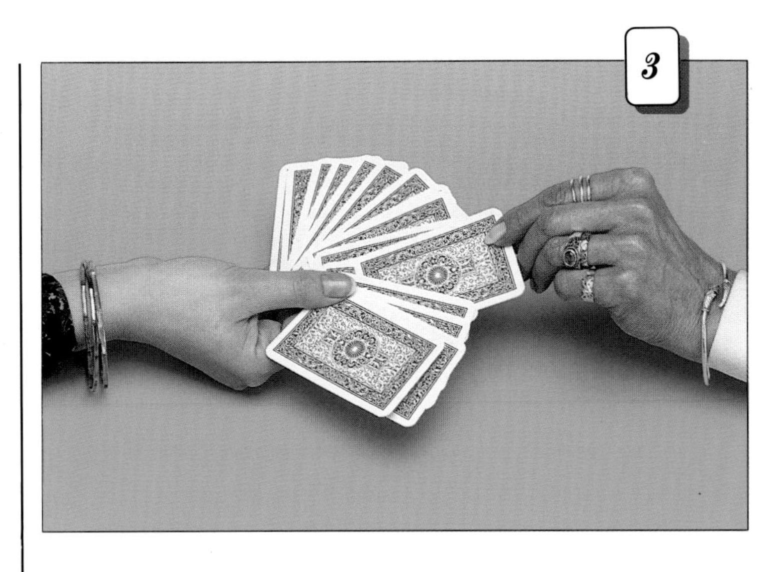

3

then fanned out, face down. From this fan, the Enquirer selects a client card, notes its value and replaces it, face down, and according to personal choice, anywhere in the fan (**3**).

You may wonder what happens if a male Enquirer selects a Queen as a client card, or a female enquirer a client card with a male identity. Do remember that we all comprise both feminine and masculine elements in our natures, and that the selection of an ostensibly "female" card in no way reflects on the "masculinity" of the Enquirer. It simply means that the feminine aspect of the Enquirer's nature, i.e. receptiveness, intuitiveness and introspectiveness, is emphasized.

The Reader carefully gathers the cards together and lays them out, face up, in the formal Fan spread (**4**, **5**,). The client card should be among the first thirteen laid out; if not, card seven of the same

4

suit will suffice. If neither of these cards is present, it should be accepted that these cards choose to remain silent, or the Reader must begin again. Cards fourteen to eighteen are placed left to right, in a straight line, directly under cards one to thirteen (**6**).

Examining cards one to thirteen, the client card is found and is the first to be read. Moving right and counting the client card as number one, read card number five. Still moving right and counting the second interpreted card as number one, read the next fifth card. Depending on the position of the client card, it may be necessary to continue from card thirteen and move left to the beginning of the fan, to complete a group of five cards. The sequence of three readings should end at the card lying before the client card. Of the five cards below the Fan, cards fourteen and eighteen are interpreted together, then cards fifteen and seventeen and finally, card sixteen.

READING THE FAN

Liz, the Enquirer, is a PR consultant in her late twenties. Her career has not provided Liz with the success and happiness for which she had hoped. Physically and emotionally, she remains unfulfilled and asks: *"Is there something more for me – hopefully, in the near future?"*

THE IMMEDIATE PICTURE

An immediate assessment of the Fan lay-out reveals a predominance of black cards over red. Not an encouraging outlook for Liz. However, the nine of Hearts, the "heart's desire" card, lying at the side of the client card, ensures that Liz's destiny is all that she could wish it to be!

INTERPRETATION

The first stage of the interpretation involves a reading of the client card (Card One) and Cards Two and Three in the Fan.

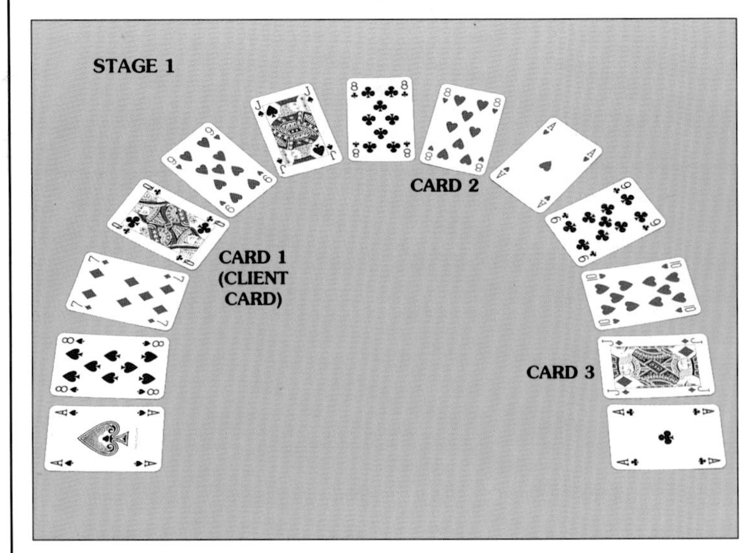

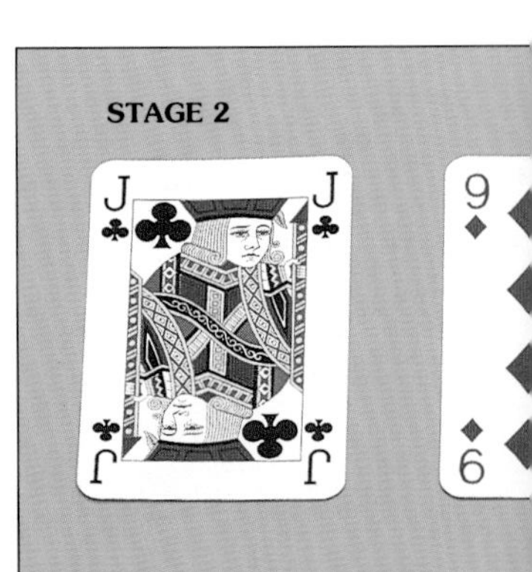

Card One: The Queen of Clubs Representing Liz, this card could not have been more appropriate since Liz herself is a warm, vital person; attractive and intelligent and the envy of her female colleagues. Money and the luxuries it can buy figure highly in the scheme of things for Liz – the wealthier her boyfriends are, the more attractive they become!

Card Two: The Eight of Hearts It is make-or-break time with an affair of the heart. Liz's latest boyfriend resents being used as a meal ticket and threatens to walk out? Liz is fast running out of lovers and her reputation as a gold digger does not help. Men avoid her.

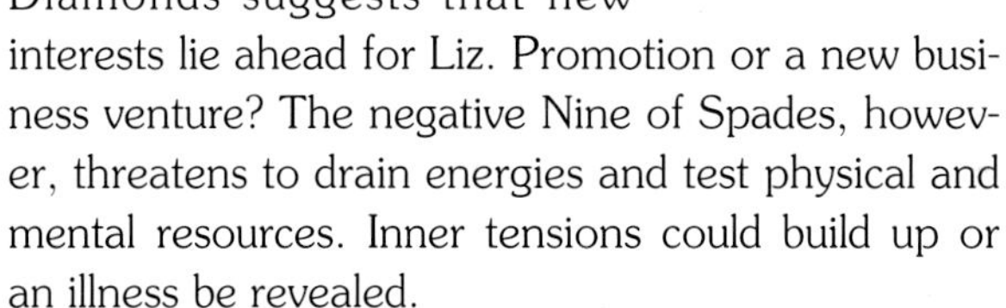

Card Three: The Jack of Diamonds reversed A fair-haired person presents himself. A stubborn unreliable young man, or an immature male colleague who is ambitious but whose lack of know-how means he will never be a success? Either way, Liz would be well-advised to steer clear of this potential troublemaker!

STAGE TWO

With regard to the five cards below the Fan, cards fourteen and eighteen are interpreted together; cards fifteen and seventeen follow and, finally, card sixteen is interpreted.

Cards Fourteen and Eighteen: The Jack of Clubs and the Seven of Spades There is indication of either an enterprising youth with more ambition than talent, or a brown-haired apathetic adult male with decreased energy drives whose plans remain unrealized. The Seven of Spades brings gloom and despondency to the situation and also an unwillingness to accept life's ups and downs philosophically.

Cards Fifteen and Seventeen: The Nine of Diamonds and the Nine of Spades The Nine of Diamonds suggests that new interests lie ahead for Liz. Promotion or a new business venture? The negative Nine of Spades, however, threatens to drain energies and test physical and mental resources. Inner tensions could build up or an illness be revealed.

Card Sixteen: The King of Clubs A mature, generous man, well-respected in business circles, has bold, imaginative plans bringing much personal wealth. Financial gain generally is predicted since this King lies between two Nines, indicating that a change professionally could lead to monetary advantage.

SUMMARY

Liz waves goodbye to her latest boyfriend. An unpleasant character admires her wit and intellect but she should avoid him at all costs. There is a brown-haired man who is depressed and in need of emotional support; a new challenge or opportunity presents itself to Liz. A supportive relationship with the man whose plans have failed to succeed? Efforts here come to nothing; her partner's loss of drive and increasing sense of desolation become too much, even for lively Liz. For her, life improves – in the reassuring shape of a mature, wealthy, generous man, well-respected in his professional sphere, which is probably finance. Resourceful Liz teams up with her Mr. Right. Her client card, the Queen of Clubs, holds a strong and positive connection with the King of Clubs, promising a warm, wealthy relationship in both physical and emotional aspects for Liz and her new partner.

THE GYPSY FORTUNE

Said to have originated in the Balkans, the Gypsy Fortune spread is still widely used by European gypsies today, its simple yet highly personal message bringing fullest expression to that which lies close to the Enquirer's heart . . .

THE WISDOM OF THE WANDERERS

The name "gypsy" is an abbreviation of "Egyptian" and describes a sect of wandering folk who travelled the Mediterranean area and south-east Europe during the Middle Ages. Purveyors of a rich, exotic tribal wisdom, culled from the countries through which they journeyed, gypsy lore perhaps had its basic tenets in the Hindu and Kabbalistic religions. The gypsies refer to themselves as Romané and their language as Romani-tchib, tchib meaning tongue. The gypsy race, heirs to a vast treasury of arcane knowledge, are practised in the art of fortune-telling and, it is said, hypnosis and the ability to "charm" away sickness or evil spirits. Chiromancy or palmistry is also an art for which the Romany is renowned. Though gypsies are not known to have practised astrology, some sources hold that the three Magi who followed the Star to Bethlehem were gypsies.

From their earliest known links with "eastern" or Chaldean beliefs and religion, to the wandering folk living by their own unique brand of occult lore, the Gypsy Fortune spread reflects the "magic" of the old Romany ways and through the cards, enables Enquirers to heed the secrets hidden in their souls.

SELECTING THE CARDS

The Gypsy Fortune offers deep insight into the personal life of the Enquirer; however, for this spread, a client card is not required. The top line represents the past; the middle line the present; and the third line, the future. . . *The Gypsy Fortune reveals inner secrets; heart's desires; true love; health; wealth and happiness . . .*

Fan the 52-card deck face down on the table and invite the Enquirer to select seven cards, using the left hand (**1**). Each of the cards should be passed to the Reader who accepts them with the right hand (**2**), placing them in a pile to the left. This ritual occurs three times giving three piles.

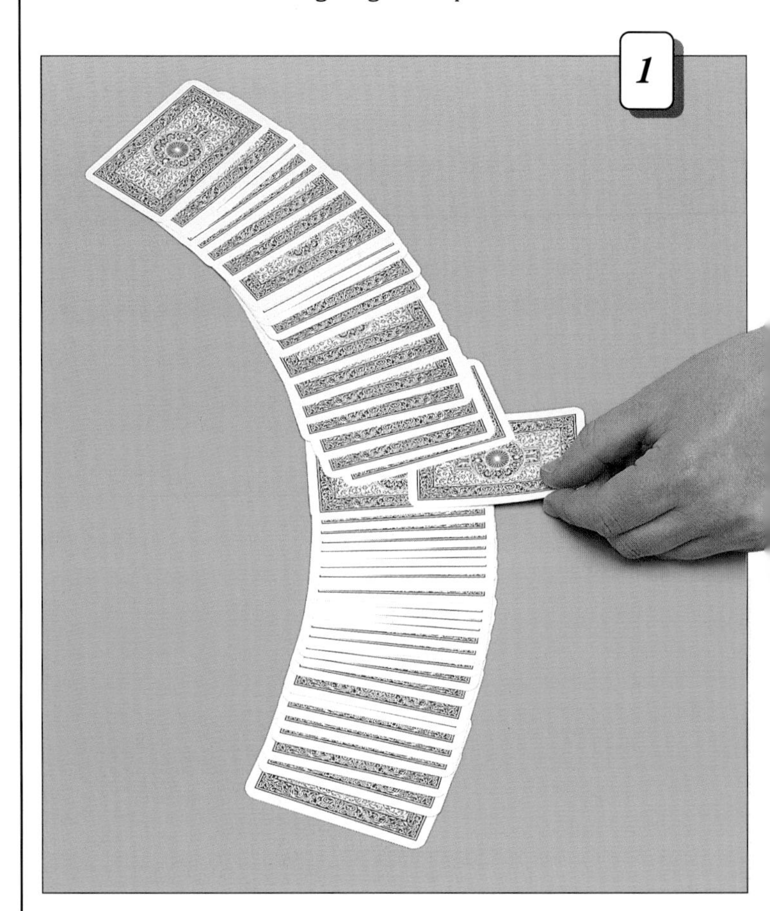

The Reader takes the first pile of cards and turns it over (**3**), so that the first card placed is the first one selected by the Enquirer. Seven cards are laid out from left to right, as seen below (**4**). The Reader repeats this sequence with the second and third piles of cards, making three lines in all (**5**). The cards are interpreted left to right, starting with the top line.

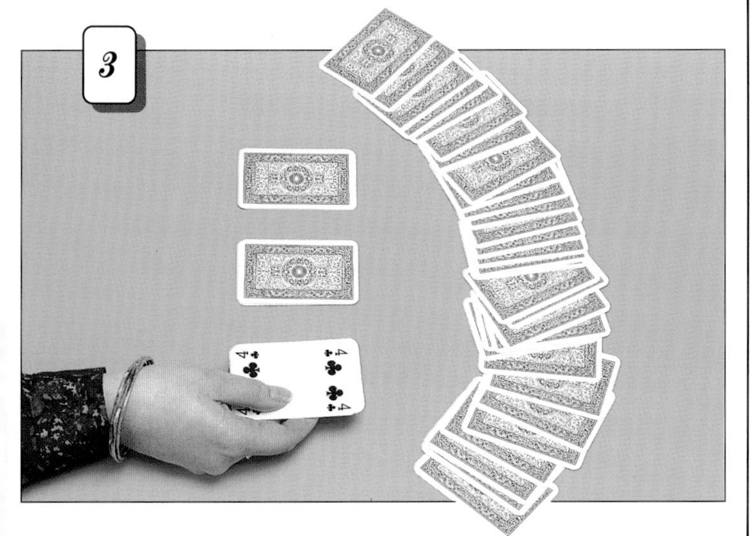

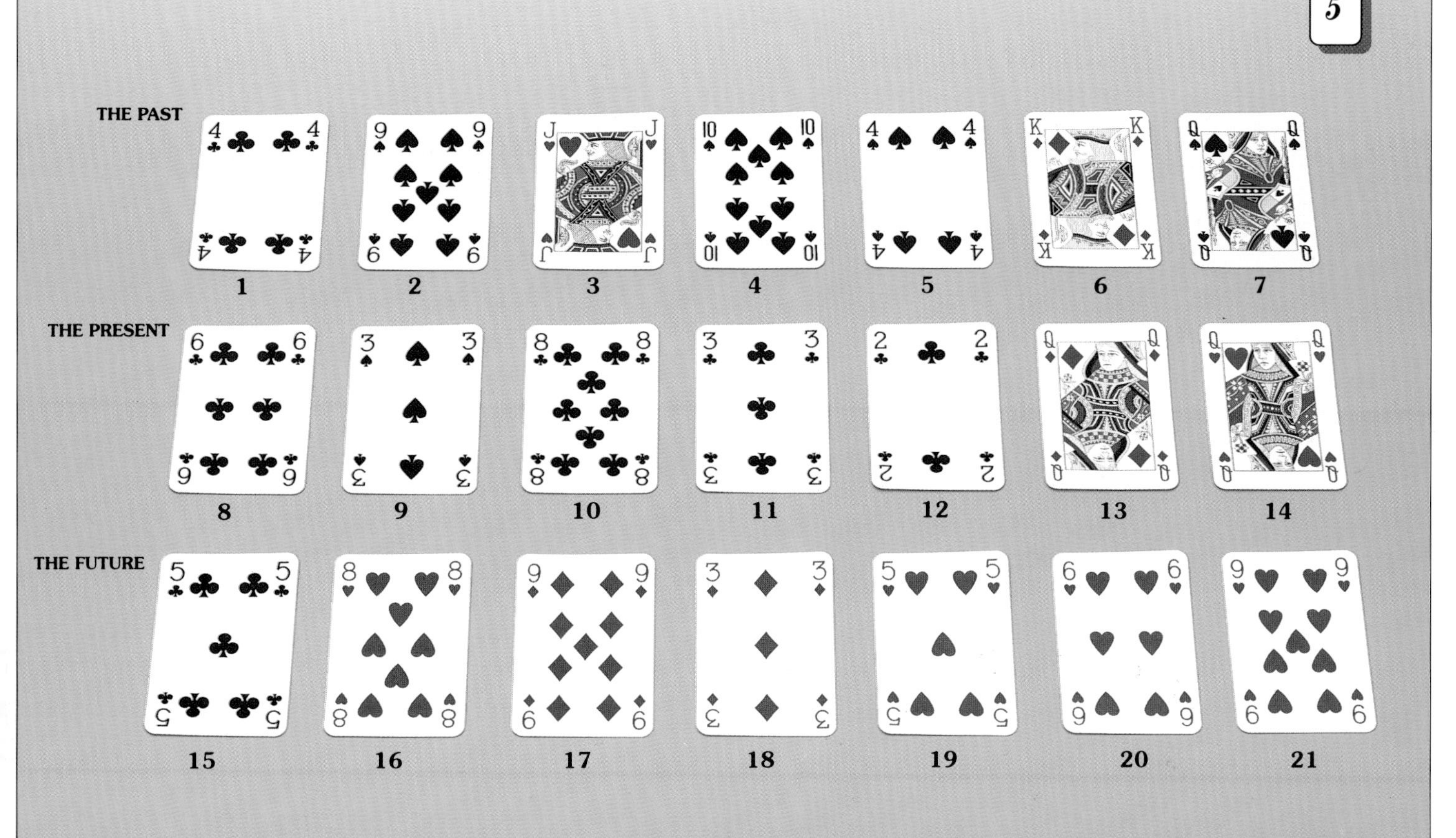

READING THE GYPSY FORTUNE

Matthew, the Enquirer, is a bright, though sensitive, young man recently graduated from University. He came into a small inheritance and entered a business partnership with a more experienced, older man. However, crossed in love, emotions wreak havoc with Matthew's grasp on reality . . . In despair he asks: *"What hope is there for my future?"* The cards outline Matthew's story . . .

Four of Clubs Balance and harmony in the business relationship were in question – perhaps following the loss of personal items, such as keys or cash?

Nine of Spades This negative card indicates that there was a draining of energies following this incident. Physical and mental resources were put to the test and inner tensions built up.

Jack of Hearts reversed Matters worsened as Matthew appears to have been rejected by his girlfriend. Badly hurt, he gave way to prolonged bouts of self-pity.

THE PAST

Ten of Spades reversed Despondency set in. Emotional stability was at risk.

Four of Spades reversed Business matters were neglected. Avoidance and delaying tactics caused more problems for Matthew.

King of Diamonds reversed A fair-haired man, probably Matthew's partner, caused a bitter dispute. Devious deceptions and discrepancies were revealed.

Queen of Spades reversed A spiteful, dark-haired

woman, probably the partner's wife, castigated Matthew for their dire straits, crushing him with her vindictive words. Matthew descended further into despondency and despair.

THE PRESENT

Six of Clubs reversed In an effort to recoup losses, Matthew resorts to gambling with disastrous financial results.

Three of Spades Financial security is severely threatened. Actions by creditors – one in particular – cause trouble.

Eight of Clubs Increased anxiety over financial affairs. More "easy" money-making schemes go wrong.

Three of Clubs reversed Self-recrimination follows. Matthew despairs but lacks the drive to improve matters.

Two of Clubs reversed Bitter back-biting by Matthew's partner destroys whatever initiative and drive remain. The relationship collapses.

Queen of Diamonds reversed Through malicious gossip, the former partner's wife makes life unbearable for Matthew.

Queen of Hearts reversed A supportive, romantic partner in Matthew's life becomes aggrieved and dreams of how things could be. She grows tired of the way things are.

THE FUTURE

Five of Clubs reversed The gambling appears to continue . . .

Eight of Hearts reversed Matthew's girlfriend increasingly tires of the situation. There are arguments and recriminations.

Nine of Diamonds reversed Matthew's attempt to relinquish his gambling ways will fail. Energies diminish further. Deep despondency.

Three of Diamonds reversed Lack of drive dashes hopes of recovery.

Five of Hearts Matters on the home front will require careful handling. Impassioned outbursts could lead to misunderstandings. Get-rich-quick ideas are to be discouraged.

Six of Hearts Heart's desires lie ahead? All is possible – at a price. Acceptable compromise, self-sacrifice and determined effort will be called for. Matthew seeks professional help with his problem?

Nine of Hearts The "heart's desire" card! Following sincere effort, Matthew's dreams *could* come true! His girlfriend will again offer her heartfelt support and future plans for both look most optimistic . . .

SUMMARY

The gradual decline of Matthew's fortunes is clearly outlined by the cards. His Past indicates a partnership deadlock (two Fours) and highlights the appearance of a vindictive woman (Queen of Spades). The Present holds a promising outlook (two Threes) but harmful gossip between two friends is likely (two Queens). The Future predicts that Matthew and his lover will still be at odds (two Fives) but that a minor change professionally could bring financial gain (two Nines). Finally, the Nine of Hearts promises that Matthew could fulfil his heart's desires!

THE WEEKLY FORECAST

The Weekly Forecast is the spread to use when an Enquirer asks a question with regard to the coming week. Is a career or domestic crisis imminent? Is an important interview or meeting about to take place? Self-knowledge is the key which helps us to control our lives. Divination is the tool which turns the key of the door to self-enlightenment. The Weekly Forecast is a particularly potent, short-term prediction for the Enquirer who is anxious to learn what the immediate seven days are about to bring.

LAYING DOWN THE CARDS

Shuffle the 32-card deck thoroughly (**1**) and cut once to the left using the left hand. Place the two piles together and shuffle the deck again. From left to right, lay out the first seven cards in a line, face up. These cards represent the seven days of the week from Sunday through to Saturday.

From left to right, cover these cards with the next seven cards, face down (**2**). These cards represent what each day has in store for the Enquirer during the following week. Place the next two cards in the deck on one side, face down (**3**).

With the right hand, the Reader turns up and reads each covering card (**4**) in relation to the corresponding "day" card, thus giving a day-by-day inter-

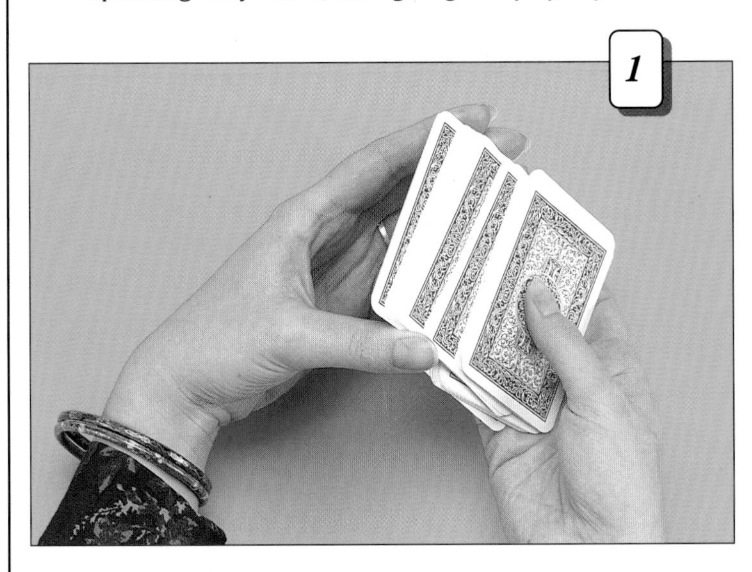

pretation of the forecast for the coming week (**5**). Note that black cards can indicate ill luck for the Enquirer or the appearance of a dark-haired person and that red cards can mean good luck for the Enquirer or the appearance of a fair-haired person. Note and interpret the combinations of cards (see pp 82-3).

Finally, turn over the two cards placed on one side, for a reading of the week as a whole (**6**). Two black cards may mean a bad week; two red cards, a good week and one of each, a mixture of both. But beware, the cards may deem otherwise!

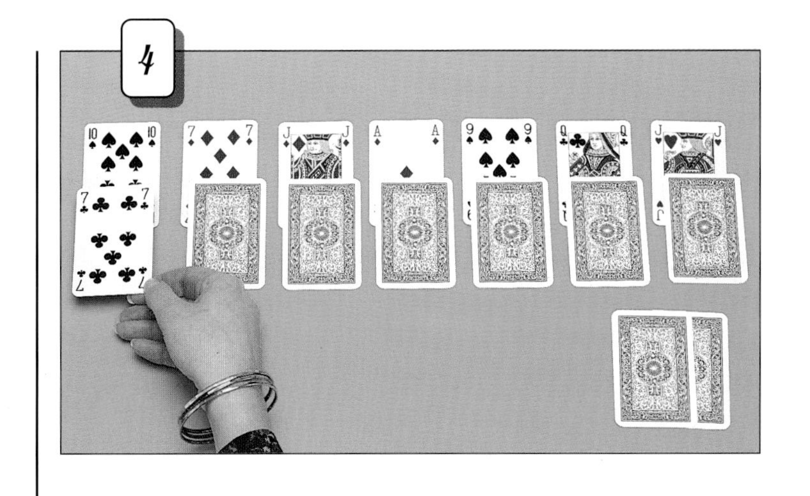

THE THREE-MONTH LUCKY THIRTEEN SPREAD

This spread gives a three-month forecast for, arguably, the three most important aspects of our lives: money, love and happiness. The number Thirteen is considered by many to hold connotations of ill luck. Others, however, including those who follow the path of Wicca, believe it to be the most benign of numbers. For this reason, I have chosen thirteen cards for this spread . . .

CREATING THE SPREAD

Shuffle and fan the 32-card deck and invite the Enquirer to select the client card. Place this card to one side, face down. The Enquirer then shuffles the remaining cards and cuts to the left, using the left hand. The two piles are gathered together and the Enquirer shuffles the deck once more. With the left hand, the cards are passed to the Reader who accepts them with the right hand.

The Reader lays out the cards as shown in the sequence, four cards representing months one, two and three successively (**1**,**2**). Cards One, Five and Nine each represent the prevailing influence of the month. The other cards in each month hold corresponding forecasts for the Enquirer's money, love and happiness prospects. The Final Word card is also the client card (previously placed to one side) and gives an intensely personal slant to the Enquirer's path forward to the following month. For advice on how to interpret cards in combination see pages 72-79 for the suits and their meanings; pages 82-3 for combinations of cards in a spread, and 84-5 for court cards, their characteristics and relationships.

Uncut playing cards dating from the late 18th century.

1

2

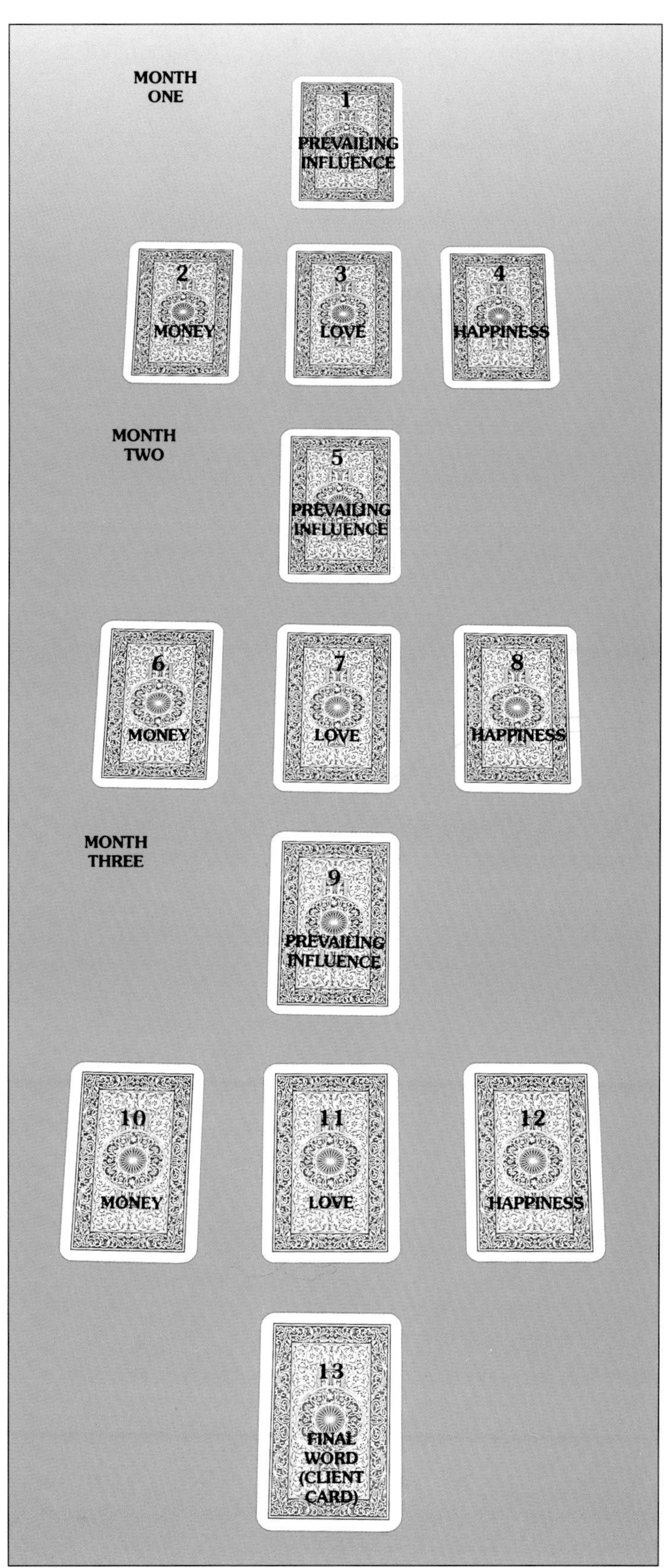
MONTH ONE
1
PREVAILING INFLUENCE
2
MONEY
3
LOVE
4
HAPPINESS
MONTH TWO
5
PREVAILING INFLUENCE
6
MONEY
7
LOVE
8
HAPPINESS
MONTH THREE
9
PREVAILING INFLUENCE
10
MONEY
11
LOVE
12
HAPPINESS
13
FINAL WORD (CLIENT CARD)

THE TWELVE ON TWELVE SPREAD

The Twelve on Twelve spread offers the Enquirer an interesting insight into both the conscious and sub-conscious aspects of his or her life, outlining the present and predicting the future.

CONSCIOUS AND SUB-CONSCIOUS

Invite the Enquirer to shuffle the 32-card deck and cut once to the left, using the left hand (**1**). The card at the bottom of pile one (i.e. the original top half of the deck) is the client card; its value should be noted (**2**) and the two piles then placed together.

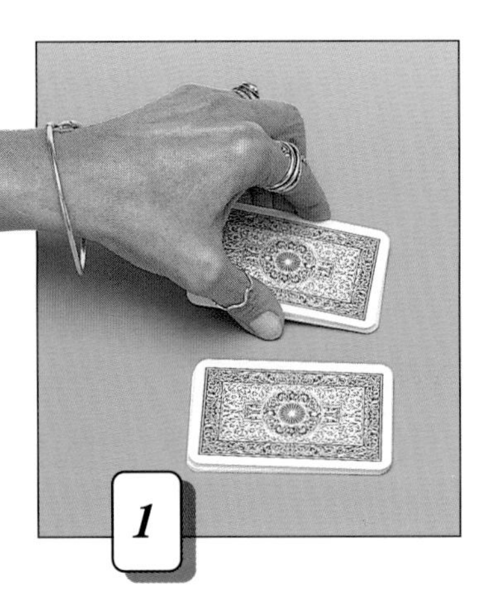

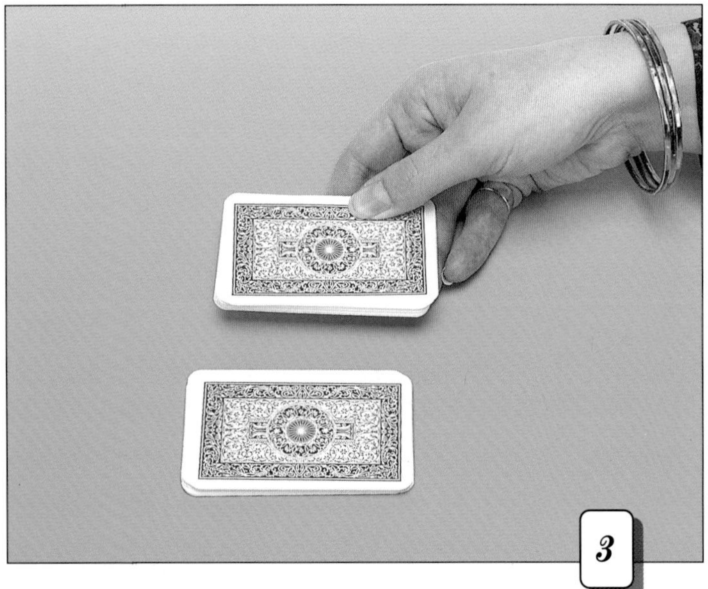

The Enquirer shuffles the deck again and cuts it to the left, using the left hand. From pile one (**3**), the Reader places the first twelve cards, left to right, face up in two rows of six (**4**). From pile two, the first twelve cards are placed on top of the corresponding first set (**5**,**6**). The cards in the first set should remain visible.

Scan the spread to find the client card, or the seven of the same suit if it is not present. If neither have appeared, they have nothing to reveal. Read each pair of cards, bearing in mind that the covering card represents the conscious or outward expression of the Enquirer and that the card underneath symbolizes the sub-conscious or inner feelings of the Enquirer. The Reader's intuitive powers should be well to the fore with this spread; if in doubt, err on the side of a less detailed reading! An example interpretation of this spread is given overleaf.

6

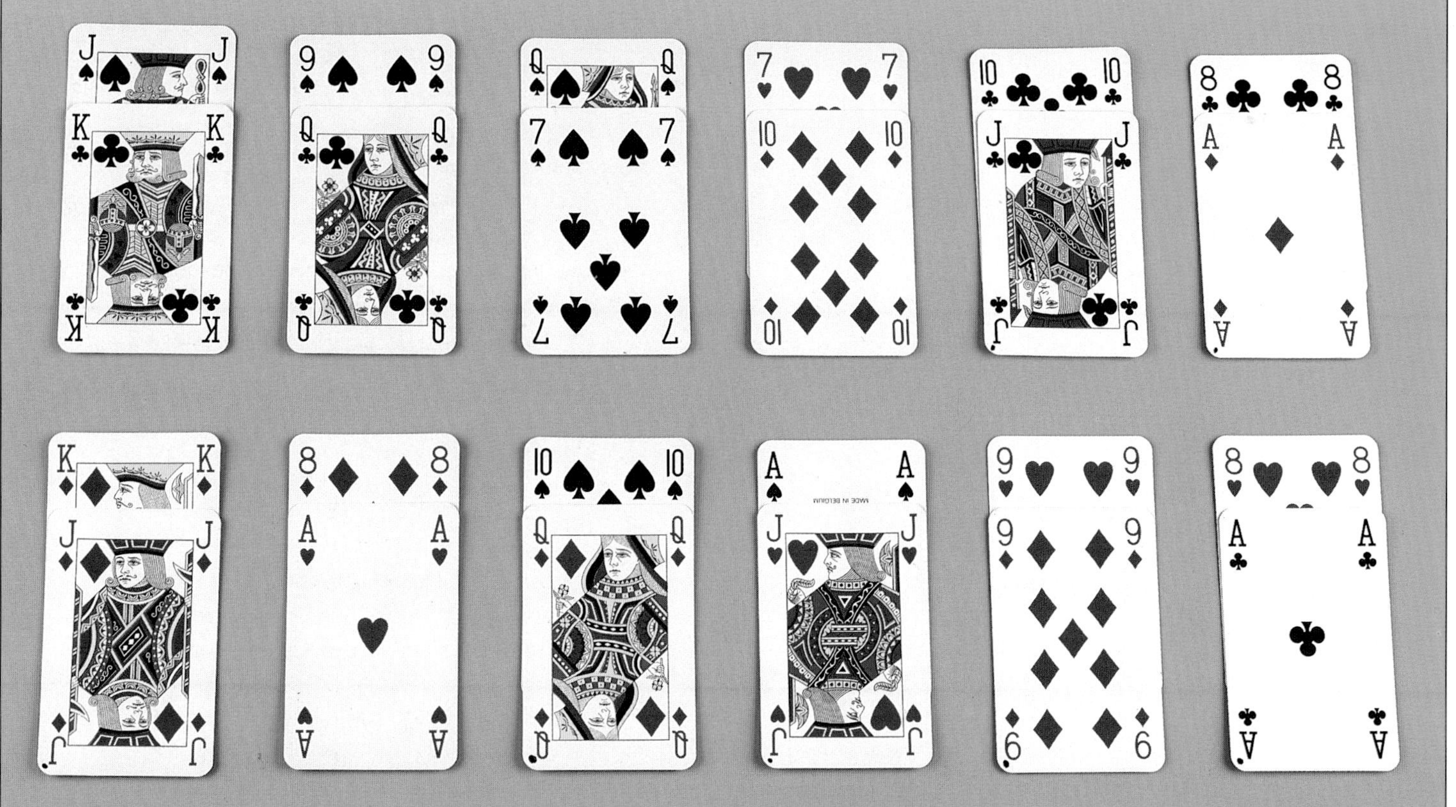

READING THE TWELVE ON TWELVE SPREAD

Jane, the Enquirer, is a young woman in her twenties. Unforthcoming and wary, she asks: *"Should I stay at home with my parents or find a place of my own?"*

INTERPRETING THE PAIRS

Pair One The King of Clubs, a warm, generous man, covers the Jack of Spades, an emotionally immature, inadequate character.

Pair Two The Queen of Clubs, a strong, intelligent, resourceful woman, used to the luxuries of life, covers the negative, draining Nine of Spades.

Pair Three The Seven of Spades, indicating secret fears, inner doubts and an unwillingness to take life philosophically, covers the Queen of Spades, an unscrupulous woman, sly and cunning. Beware.

Pair Four The Ten of Diamonds brings the threat of failure; anxiety; loss of direction and pessimism. This card covers the Seven of Hearts which holds great potential for personal happiness – providing balance and harmony exist.

Pair Five The Jack of Clubs reversed confers hot-headed drive followed by restlessness. Unreliability. Dishonesty. This card covers the Ten of Clubs. Spendthrift ways dissipate savings.

Pair Six The Ace of Diamonds reversed grants the will to win but drive and motivation is lacking. Setbacks. Projects fail. This card covers the Eight of Clubs creating anxiety over money, and warning against taking gambles at this time.

Pair Seven An unreliable person is unwilling to admit he is wrong. The misleading Jack of Diamonds reversed covers the King of Diamonds reversed. A devious schemer; deceptions revealed. A bitter dispute.

Pair Eight Client card the Ace of Hearts reveals warm family feelings; fertile beginnings; happiness in the home; good news. Do not let the heart rule the head. This card covers the Eight of Diamonds reversed. Opportunities lost through indecision. Loss of energy. Self-recrimination.

Pair Nine A spiteful woman. Malicious gossip is hurtful. The Queen of Diamonds reversed covers the Ten of Spades reversed, causing matters to deteriorate further. Problems recur.

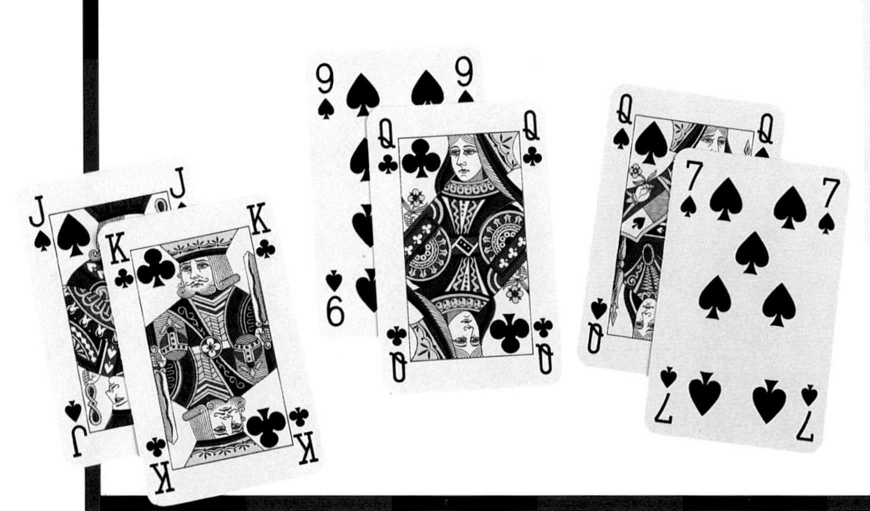

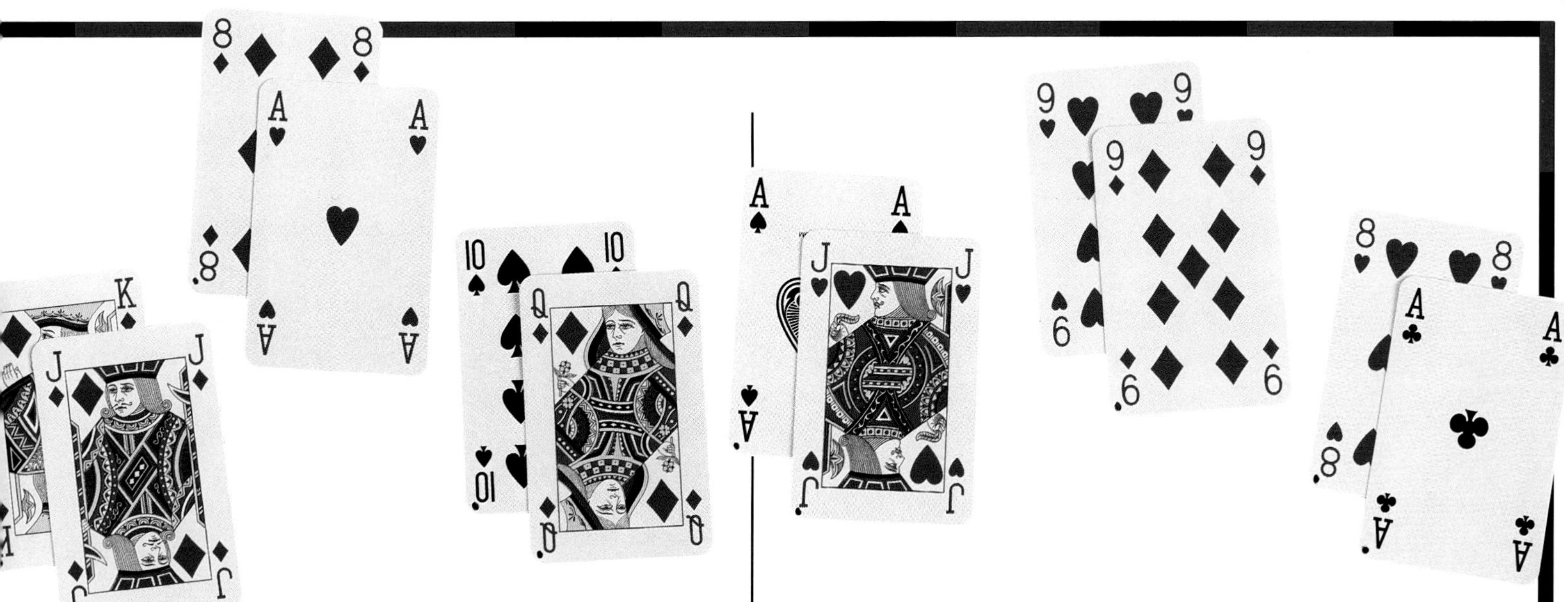

Pair Ten The Jack of Hearts reversed. A short-tempered person, rejected in love, wallows in self-pity. This card covers the Ace of Spades reversed. Disharmony and instability within emotional relationships.

Pair Eleven The Nine of Diamonds reversed brings delay; dispute and obstacles. Self-doubt saps energy. This card covers the Nine of Hearts. Dreams come true, especially relating to family.

Pair Twelve The Ace of Clubs reversed indicates financial poverty and loss of inner contentment. This card covers the Eight of Hearts reversed. Obstacles in romantic relationships. Opposition. Prejudice.

SUMMARY

Jane reveals her story which equates with the message of the cards . . . She lives with her parents; (Pair 1) a father whose bluff exterior hides an ineffectual nature; (Pair 2) a mother, vivacious and self-centred, whose happiness revolved around her luxurious home until a debilitating illness was diagnosed. (Pair 3) An aunt, jealous of her sister, undermines Jane's love for her mother with malicious rumours. (Pair 4) Anxiety at home hinders happiness for Jane. (Pair 5) An irresponsible younger brother fritters away finances. (Pair 6) He lacks the motivation to amend and (Pair 7) he will not admit to his guilt. Deceptions revealed cause bitter dispute.

(Pair 8) Happier on the home front, Jane receives a job offer from afar. Should she leave her parents to cope? Debate. Delay. The post is filled; remorse lowers energies. (Pair 9) The aunt gossips again and disharmony returns. (Pair 10) The brother's lover rejects him and more discord follows.

(Pair 11) Bravely keeping the peace, Jane's dreams of family happiness are promised. Nonetheless, she may well leave home (Pair 12) and experience financial difficulties (regarding her new home?). Additionally, there could be parental disapproval of a romantic interest.

CONCLUSION

Despite financial problems (three Tens) and sundry minor anxieties (three Eights), love triumphs (two Sevens). Malicious gossip (three Queens) leads to rifts and new alliances (four Jacks). A stable partnership (two Kings) in a successful enterprise (three Nines) results in joy and celebration (four Aces)!

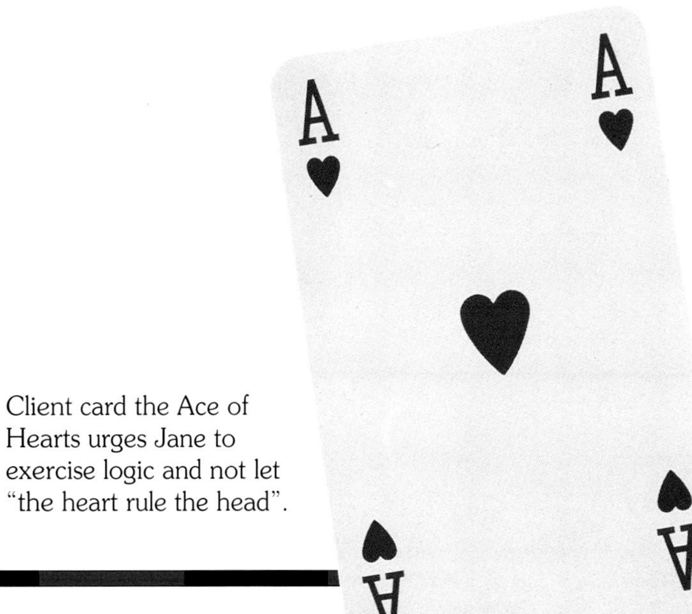

Client card the Ace of Hearts urges Jane to exercise logic and not let "the heart rule the head".

THE WHEEL OF FORTUNE

Reminiscent of the Tarot's Card Ten (X) (see page 18), the Wheel of Fortune spread symbolizes the inevitability of progress and our confrontation with Destiny as the Wheel relentlessly spins. The client card, placed at the centre of the Wheel, makes the divination of this spread a particularly powerful experience for the Enquirer.

INDICATORS OF FORTUNE

Fan the 32-card deck face down on the table and invite the Enquirer to select the client card, using the left hand (**1**). This card (**2**) is then placed, face up, in the centre of the table. The Enquirer shuffles the remaining cards and cuts twice to the left, using the left hand (**3**). Still with the left hand, the Enquirer turns over the three piles, revealing the bottom card of each pile (**4**). These are the three indicators and at this point are read by the Reader separately and in combination, giving an overall view of the Enquirer's future. These three cards have now performed their function and should be placed on one side.

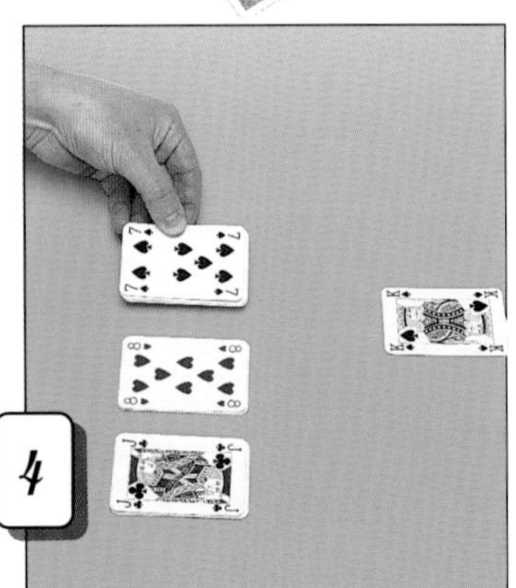

Gather the remaining cards together and starting at the position immediately above the client card, place eight cards face up and moving anti-clockwise, in a circle (**5**). Invite the Enquirer to re-shuffle the remaining cards and, working anti-clockwise, place one card under each of the original eight cards (**6**). This ritual is repeated around the circle twice (**7**,**8**) to give eight sets of three cards, each set radiating from the client card at the centre (see right).

Starting with the set positioned above the client card and moving in an anti-clockwise direction, read each set of cards. Finally, assess the spread overall, to discover further messages from the cards.

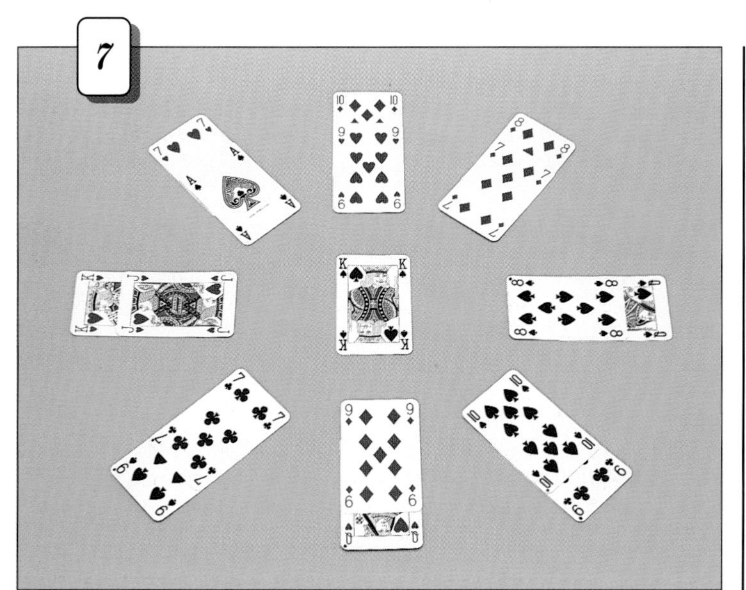
7

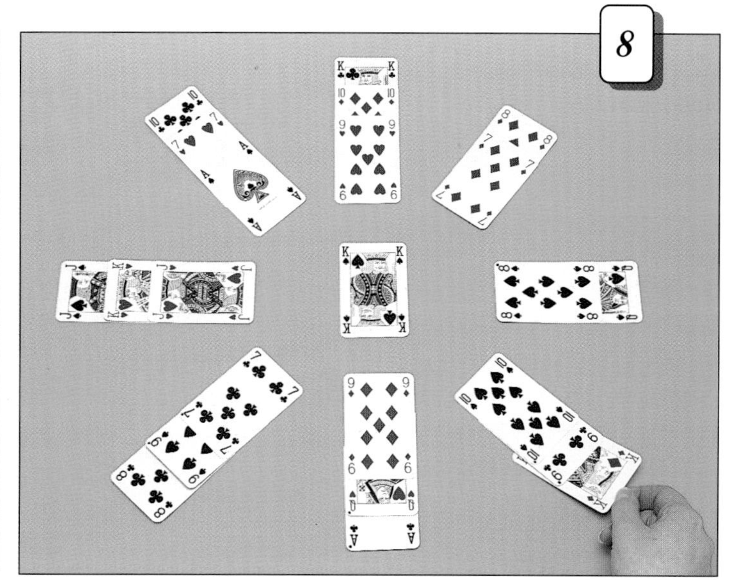
8

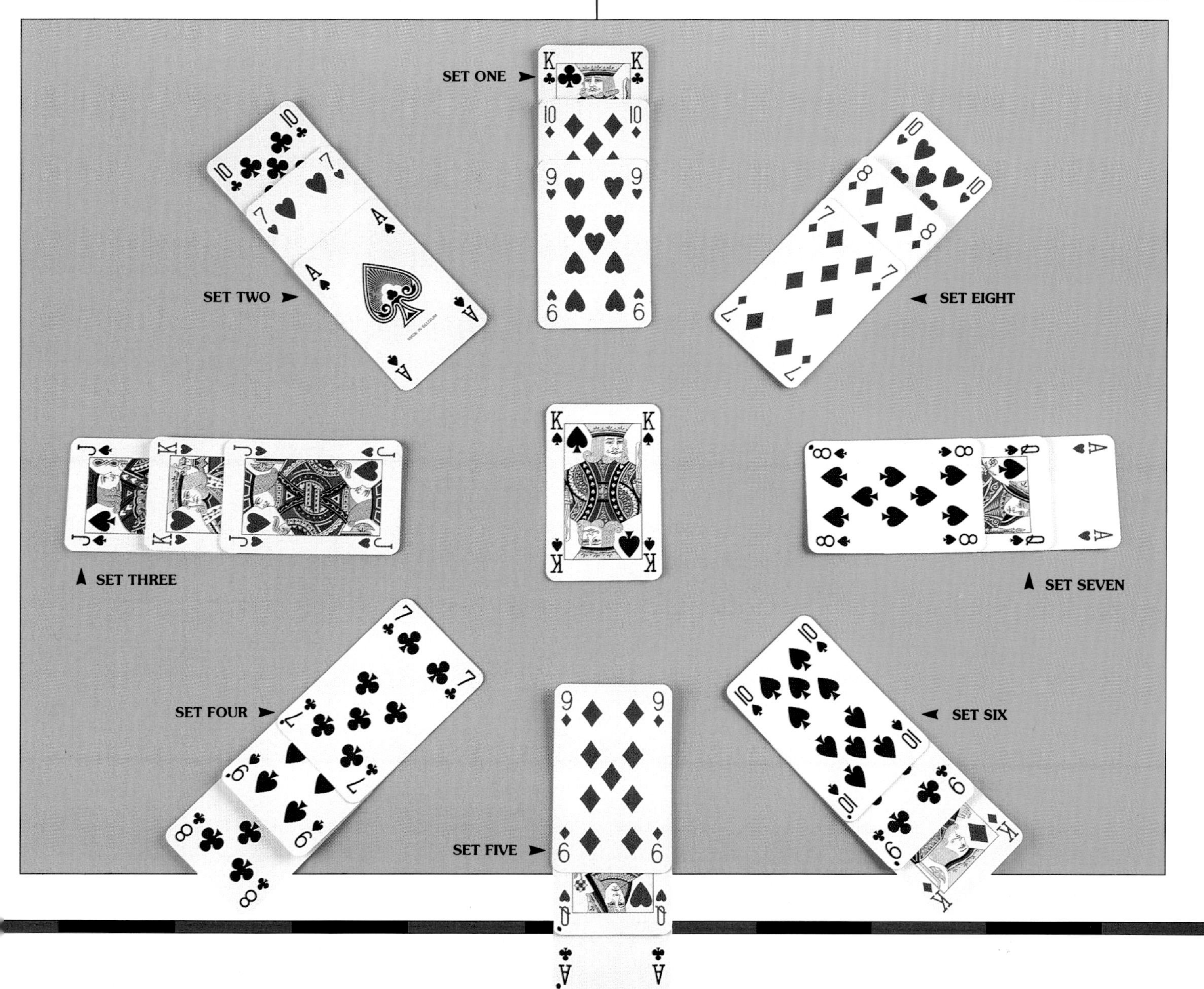
SET ONE
SET TWO
SET EIGHT
SET THREE
SET SEVEN
SET FOUR
SET SIX
SET FIVE

READING THE WHEEL OF FORTUNE

Damien, a dark-haired charismatic young actor, was anxious to learn what the future held for him. This is what the Wheel of Fortune revealed.

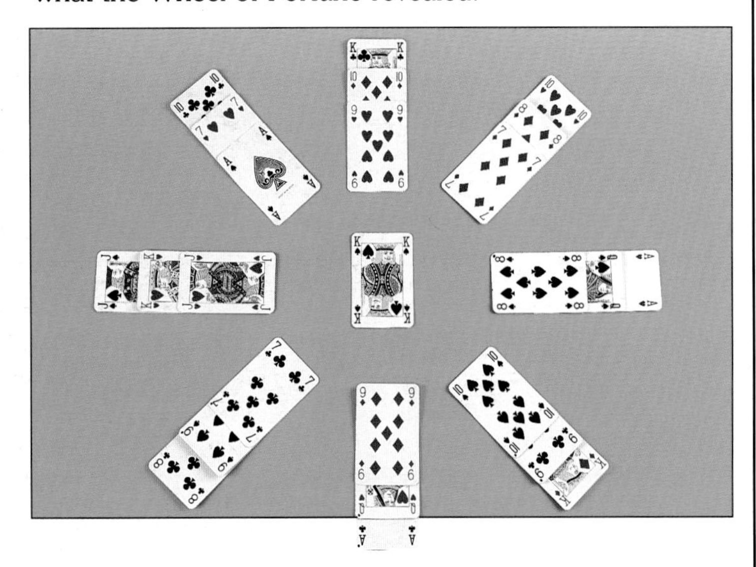

THE CLIENT CARD

Damien's unwitting selection of the King of Spades as his client card appeared to be an appropriate choice. This dynamic, authoritarian card, ruled by intellect, critical of others and showing ruthlessness in achieving its own ends, was not dissimilar to the image projected by Damien himself.

THE INDICATORS

The three indicators outline the general trend of Damien's future and indicate decreased drive (Jack of Clubs), a romantic affair troubled by the opposition and prejudice of others (Eight of Hearts), and inner doubts, gloom and despondency (Seven of Spades).

THE SETS

Set One Damien's secret wishes will come true, especially relating to romance and family (Nine of Hearts). A change involving journeys, money and career is indicated (Ten of Diamonds), but a meanness and an inability to accept change is present (King of Clubs reversed).

Set Two The end of a phase, and matters generally will come to a head (Ace of Spades). There is great potential for personal happiness (Seven of Hearts) and a substantial sum of money is likely from an unexpected source (Ten of Clubs).

Set Three Enter a friendly, fair-haired young man (Jack of Hearts) accompanied by sexual indiscretions (King of Hearts reversed). Also, a dark-haired, emotionally immature man (Jack of Spades).

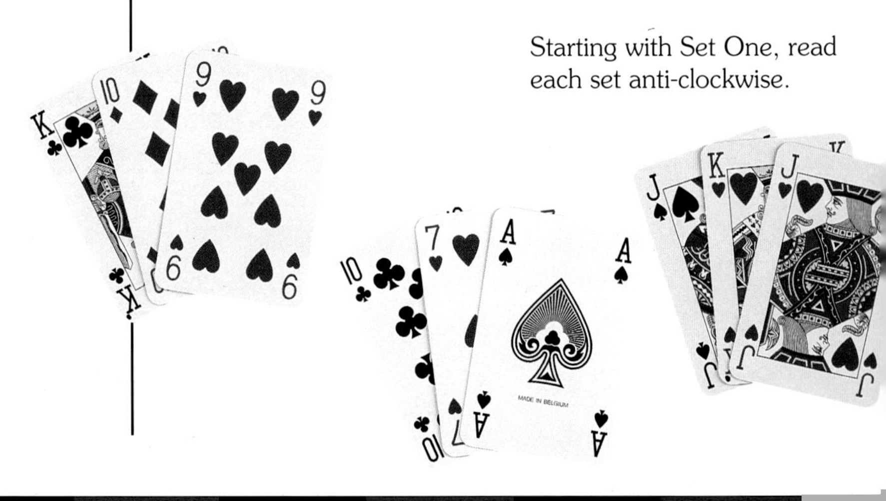

Starting with Set One, read each set anti-clockwise.

Set Four Slipshod accounting could lead to money problems (Seven of Clubs reversed). Lack of money, health problems and depression (Nine of Spades reversed). The Eight of Clubs warns against money-making ventures at this time.

Set Five Opportunities lie ahead involving career or a new business venture (Nine of Diamonds). A self-centred attitude stifles relationships (Queen of Hearts reversed). Rash money-making scheme fails (Ace of Clubs reversed).

Set Six Matters deteriorate (Ten of Spades reversed). Control of expenditure is urged (Nine of Clubs reversed). A powerful figure takes centre stage; an ambitious, fair-haired man (King of Diamonds).

Set Seven Effort comes to nothing. Despondency prevails (Eight of Spades reversed). A clever, vindictive woman could attack, verbally or otherwise (Queen of Spades reversed). New and lasting friendships. Romantic love? There is a need to control emotions (Ace of Hearts).

Set Eight Positive success. Vital energies are restored; self-confidence and material benefits flourish (Seven of Diamonds). Notwithstanding, a downturn in career and energy drives is indicated (Eight of Diamonds). A new phase; heartfelt joy and happiness; good news – the birth of a child (Ten of Hearts)?

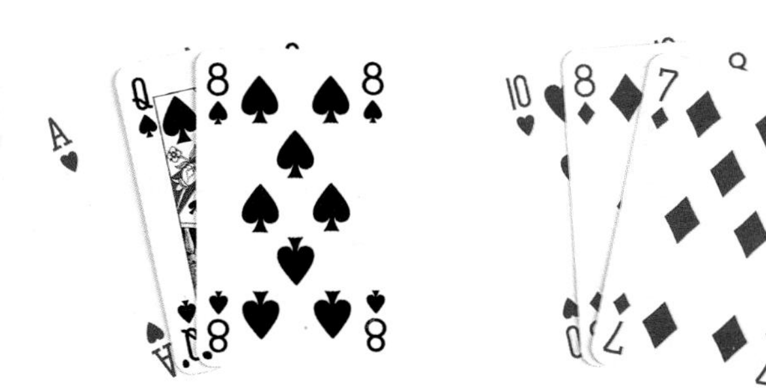

Following interpretation of the eight sets of cards are the Summary – and final Conclusion – derived from a complete reading of the Wheel of Fortune spread.

SUMMARY

Career offers from afar ensure financial security but Damien cannot adapt to changed circumstances (Set One). Matters come to a head and the arrival of a sum of money brings happiness (Set Two). Two young men appear on the scene with connotations of sexual indiscretion (Set Three). Money is lost; health matters arise and the cards warn against speculating cash at this time (Set Four). Career or business opportunities present themselves and self-ish attitudes make enemies. Risky business plans fail (Set Five). Finances are low. Damien takes on a new agent? (Set Six). Plans are thwarted; despondency prevails and a vindictive woman is best avoided. A new love interest is promised but the heart should not rule the head (Set Seven). Career success and confidence return but a set-back occurs. One cycle ends and another begins with good news and happiness on the home or romantic front (Set Eight).

CONCLUSION

Significantly placed above the client card, the Nine of Hearts augurs well for the entire reading. Despite some anxiety (four Eights) harmony prevails (four Sevens). Good fortune career-wise (four Tens) brings accolades and applause (four Kings). News of romance (Jack of Hearts next to a King) comes as a pleasant surprise (four Nines) although less-than-good news follows, (Jack of Spades *beneath* the King of Hearts which dilutes the bad news). Beware of gossip between firm friends (two Queens). Finally, the birth of a child could mean happiness and fulfilment for Damien (three Aces).

The Nine of Hearts grants heart's desires.

THE PSYCHIC SEVEN CARD SPREAD

Discover hidden personal potential with the Psychic Seven Card spread. The number Seven with its mystical "magical" links features strongly in many ancient wisdoms. The Psychic Seven Card spread discloses personal potential in a card game which reveals how we are likely to fare when meeting the challenges faced in the larger game of Life . . .

SEVEN FACETS OF SELF

The cards represent seven aspects of the Enquirer's nature. These are: Self, Heart, Positivity, Negativity, Head, Energy Drives and Tenacity.

From a fan of four court cards (Kings for a male and Queens for a female Enquirer), a client card is selected by the Enquirer. This is placed face up in the middle of the table (**1**). The Joker, Jacks and remaining Kings and Queens are excluded from the 52-card deck. Numbers 1 (Ace) to 10 in each suit remain. The Enquirer shuffles the deck thoroughly and places the cards, face down, in a pile. The Reader takes the first six cards from the top of the pile (**2**) and places each, face up, as shown (**3**,**4**).

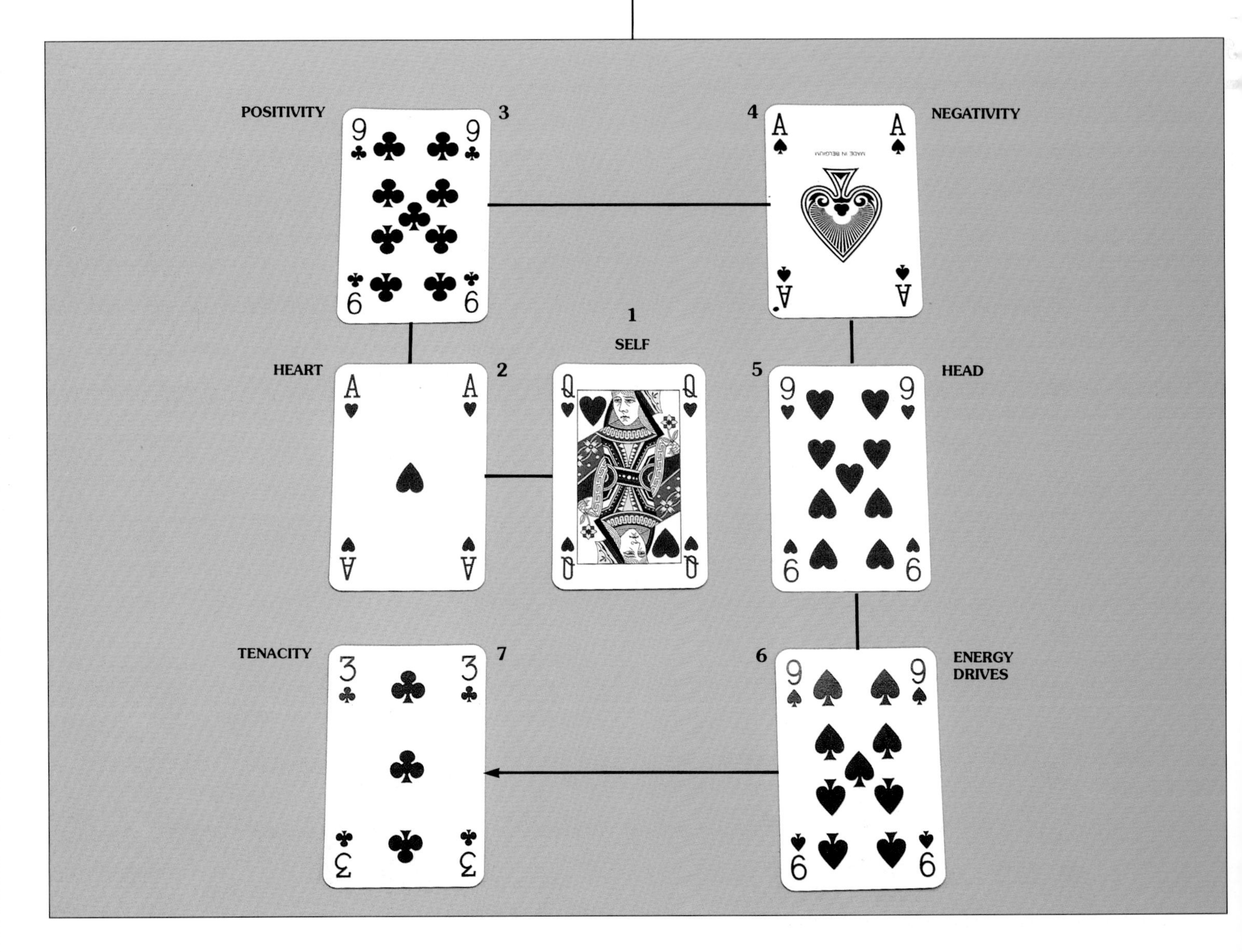

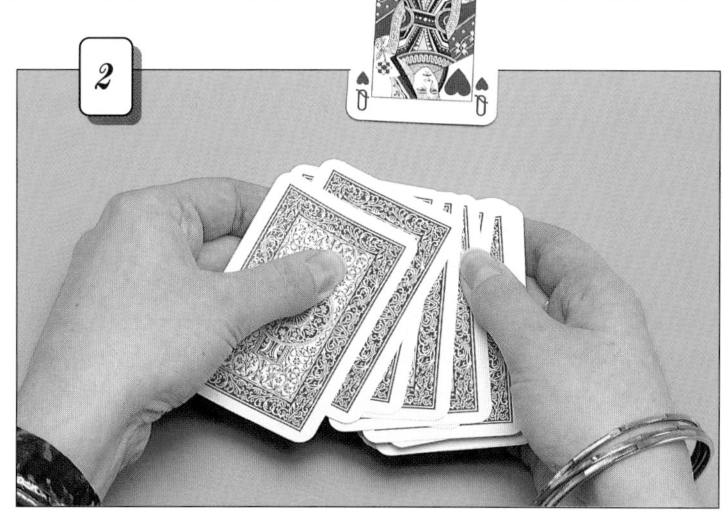

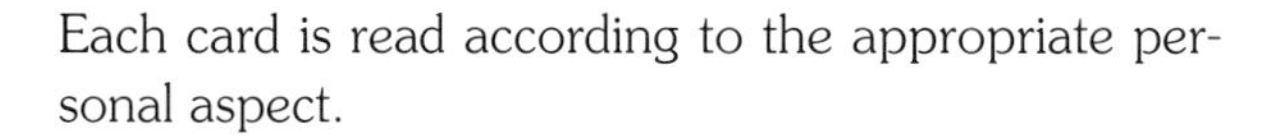

Each card is read according to the appropriate personal aspect.

SUMMARY

Card 1: Self: Queen of Hearts Sensitive and intuitive, this lady is a caring confidante to family and those seeking her help.

Card 2: Heart: Ace of Hearts Beware the heart ruling the head, especially when dealing with family.

Card 3: Positivity: Nine of Clubs Full of determination and enthusiasm, the Enquirer is at her most positive in areas of finance.

Card 4: Negativity: Ace of Spades reversed Instability within emotional relationships. A more philosophical view of life generally is urged.

Card 5: Head: Nine of Hearts This heart-warming card indicates that mental drives are family-centred in terms of hopes and desires.

Card 6: Energy Drives: Nine of Spades Energy drives are low, physically and mentally. Depression and stress-related illness possible.

Card 7: Tenacity: Three of Clubs Enthusiastic Clubs indicates financial flair and rewards. In pursuit of financial stability, great tenacity is shown.

CONCLUSION

The cycle of Seven begins and ends on an optimistic note, auguring well for the personal potential – and prospects – of the Enquirer; providing there is balance in other areas.

THE SIX-MONTH FORECAST

The Six-Month Forecast highlights the near-future fortunes of partners, applying equally to partnerships in both the business and domestic fields. Month One represents the month following that in which the reading is given.

SETTING OUT THE SPREAD

The Enquirer is invited to shuffle the 52-card deck plus the Joker thoroughly and cut once, to the left. From the first pile, the Reader places the top six cards (**1**) as shown (**2**) (Set One). This set represents the Enquirer.

From the second pile, the top six cards are also laid out as shown (**3**) (Set Two). This set represents the Enquirer's partner. The cards are then interpreted by the Reader in pairs, i.e. Month One from Sets One and Two consecutively. This reading represents the combined future fortunes of both the Enquirer and his or her partner for the immediate six-month period.

The Enquirer, John, wishes to discover the future potential of the business he has recently set up with his friend, Andrew. Although the reading is limited, the main trend of events over the immediate six months is clearly shown. In each month's reading, the first card dealt with represents the Enquirer.

Month One (Red Joker) John is in for a surprise! An affair of the heart will unexpectedly backfire, forcing him to see matters in a completely different light! (Seven of Spades) Meanwhile, Andrew has

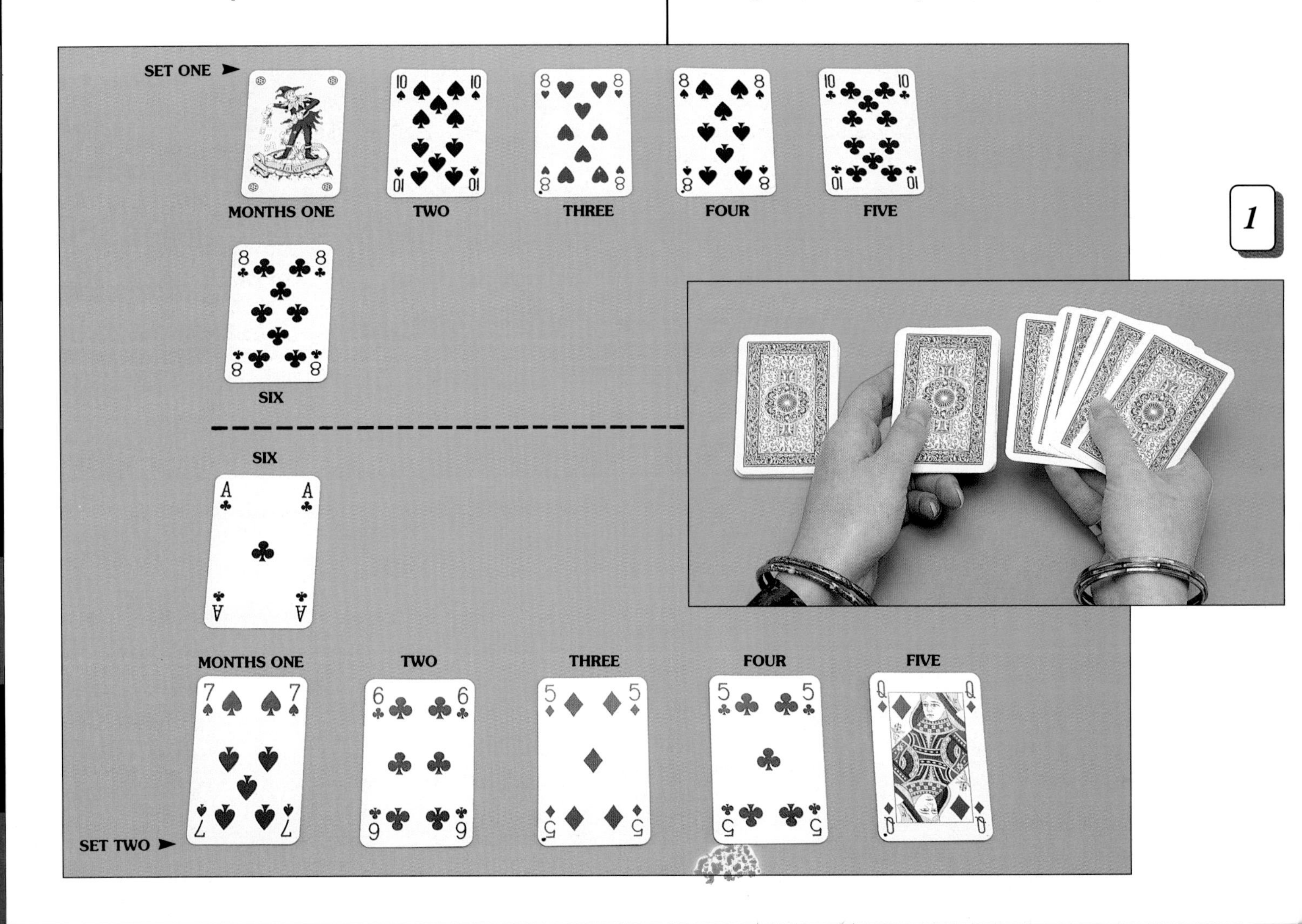

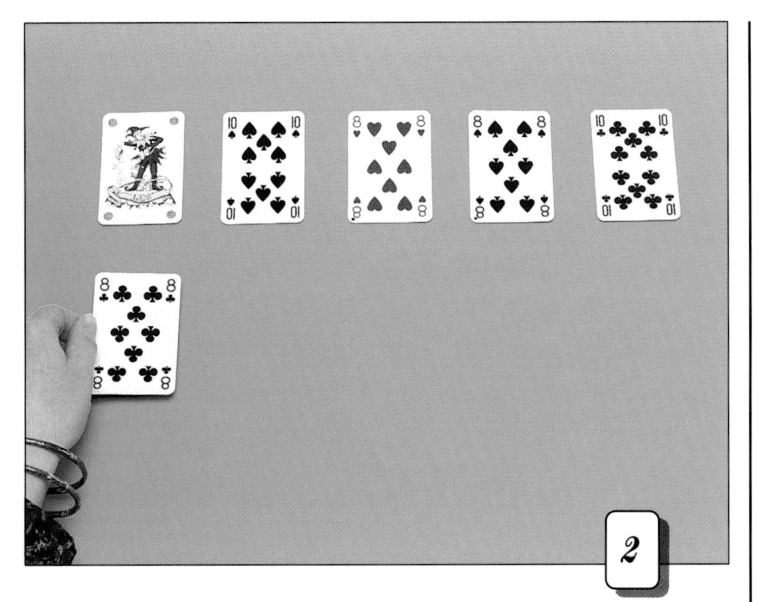

2

3

doubts and reservations, probably about the business, at this time. Are John's emotional problems affecting his business performance?

Month Two (Ten of Spades) John reaches the end of a difficult phase. Personal bitterness and frustration are felt. He blames himself for his partner's pessimism? (Six of Clubs) Andrew renews efforts in the business. Careful planning and hard work bring unavoidable stress but business is buoyant. A cash loan is possible.

Month Three (Eight of Hearts reversed) There are still problems with John's romantic involvement and he is faced with damaging opposition from a certain quarter. (Five of Diamonds reversed) Andrew's despondency returns and he may feel reluctant to continue.

Month Four (Eight of Spades reversed) Despite his efforts, nothing seems to go right for John. (Five of Clubs) Nonetheless, he and Andrew persevere. A new business direction promises profits? Or, is there a personal inheritance for Andrew?

Month Five (Ten of Clubs) One phase finishes and another commences for John with the promise of a substantial sum of money, probably from an unexpected source. (Queen of Diamonds reversed) Andrew, however, suffers as a result of malicious gossip by a spiteful woman or perhaps from a raw deal in a libel action?

Month Six (Eight of Clubs) John should avoid speculating on money-making schemes at this time. (Ace of Clubs) For Andrew, energy drives could produce substantial material or spiritual gains, though a tendency to easy-going attitudes should be discouraged. Rewards could also include those of public recognition.

Conclusion Mainly black cards in the spread rightly suggest the reading concerns "masculine activities". Unexpected upheaval in an emotional affair upsets John (Red Joker) causing friction between the two partners (two Fives). Finally, minor problems could tip the balance (three Eights) as a change of scene, perhaps of career, is indicated for John (two Tens).

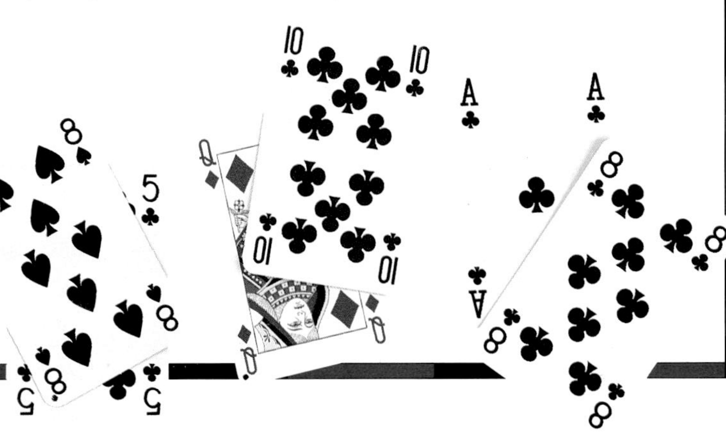

THE 13-CARD PYRAMID OF ISIS

"I am that which is, has been and will be . . ." Isis. Sister and wife of Osiris, the Egyptian deity Isis was identified with the Roman Juno, and the Greek goddesses Aphrodite and Astarte. Astarte was also revered as a Moon goddess. The Pyramid of Isis spread is ideally suited to the female querent and in it we "lift the veil of Isis" to reveal the inner nature of the Enquirer. The thirteen cards, which are laid out in a pyramid shape as illustrated, represent the 13 lunar months of the year which is also the time scale dealt with in the reading.

1

2

3

THE LINES OF THE PYRAMID

Line One (Past) outlines *What has been*, Line Two (Present), *What is*, and Line Three (Future), *What will be*. The apex of the pyramid consists of Card 13, this card represents the Final Word on the Enquirer's future.

The Enquirer is invited to shuffle the 52-card deck thoroughly and cut once, to the left. As no client card is required for this spread, the Reader then lays out thirteen cards, face up, in the order as shown (**1-3**). Forming a pyramid, each line is placed from the left, starting with Line One. The reading of each line also commences from the left.

THE INTERPRETATION

(Past) What has been . . . Some nine months ago, the Enquirer reached the end of a phase; a new one began, probably a change of career. A journey may have been involved with this change (Ten of Diamonds reversed). Goals were achieved in practical matters by dint of judicious planning. Documents signed at this time required careful scrutiny (Six of Diamonds). Health problems and depression were stressed. Financial loss and feelings of rejection made matters worse (Nine of Spades reversed). A love affair brought heartache (Seven of Hearts reversed) and family arguments led to wasted romantic opportunities (Ten of Hearts reversed). All that

the heart desired then transpired for the Enquirer. A new emotional relationship sprang into being – with the message that the heart must not rule the head (Ace of Hearts).

(Present) What is . . . Someone interferes bringing emotional upset. Alternatively, this could mean a threat to financial security. The Enquirer should be wary of third business partners or a troublesome person (Three of Spades). Difficult decisions relating to practical matters are in the offing and indecision leads to insecurity (Four of Diamonds). Sadly, a partnership ends but there is optimism for the future (Two of Spades). Harmony in business relationships is emphasized and care should be taken regarding personal items (Four of Clubs).

(Future) What will be . . . Positive success lies ahead and vital energies combined with practicality bring material benefits and enhance self-confidence (Seven of Diamonds). Problems in emotional matters are also indicated in this line (Eight of Hearts reversed).

The Final Word Yes, there is considerable potential for financial wealth in this reading, accompanied by the necessary drive to achieve that potential. Rewards may be in the shape of a gift or prize of a substantial nature. Public recognition on physical or spiritual levels could be part of this. The Enquirer is reminded not to lose sight of spiritual needs in a sometimes burning enthusiasm to achieve physical gain (Ace of Clubs).

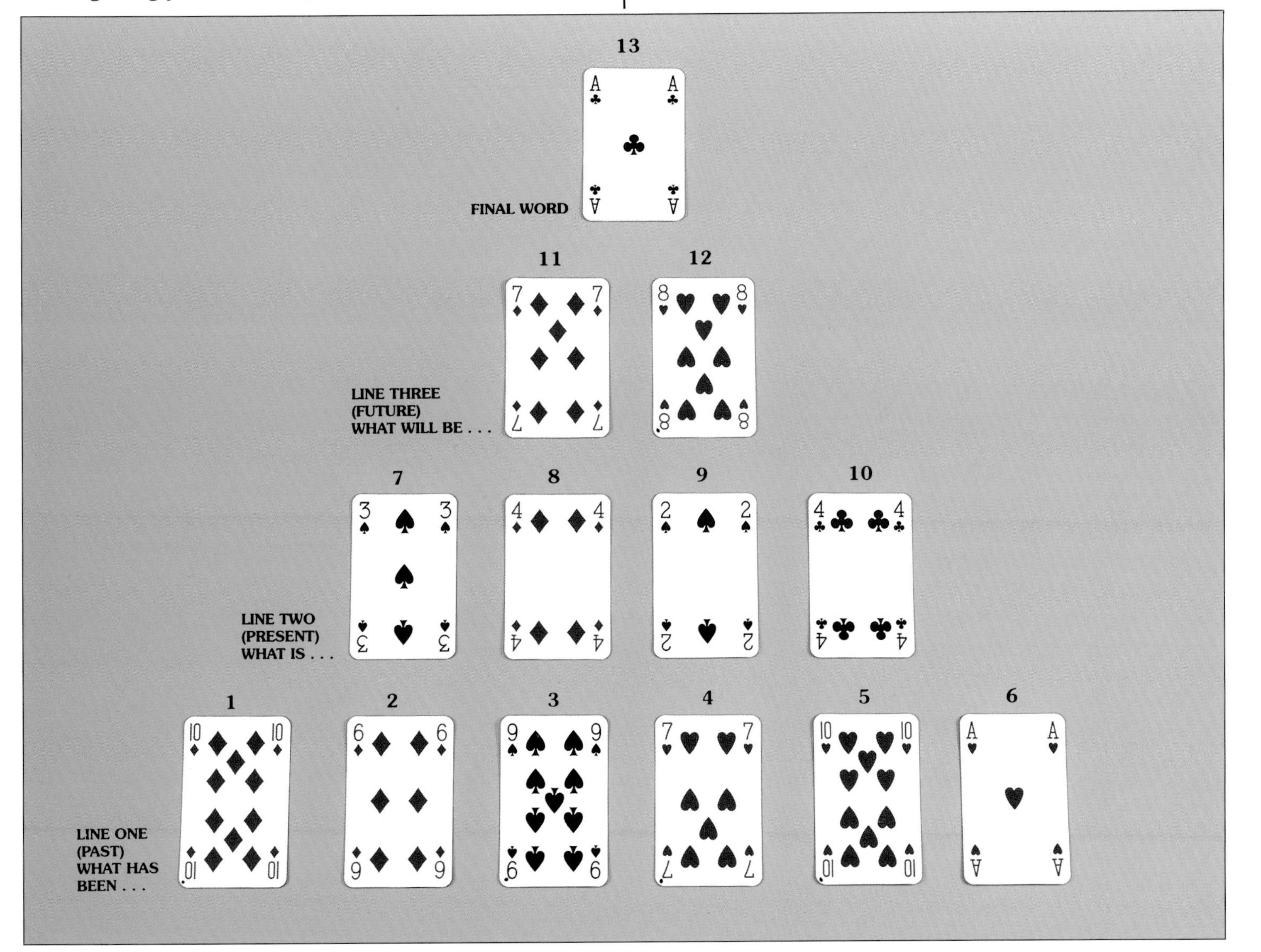

THE COSMIC SYMMETRY OF NUMBERS

Throughout Time, countless methods of prediction have been employed, enabling man's destiny to be foretold. The use of numbers as a tool of divination is just one of those many arcane ways. Showing the magical interaction of numbers and representing a microcosm of man's past, present and future, the playing cards reveal amazing links with the forces of nature.

THE SYMBOLISM OF CARDS

Said to represent Time itself, the 52-card deck reflects this cosmic relationship in the following examples illustrated. The four suits symbolize the four astrological elements, the four seasons, the four weeks in a lunar month, and the four "humours" – a term indicating a person's physical and mental disposition, designated by ancient philosophers as choleric, sanguine, phlegmatic or melancholic. The 12 court cards symbolize the twelve months in the year while the 13 cards in each suit represent the thirteen lunar months of the year. Multiply the seven days of the week by 52 (the full deck and weeks in the year) and you get a total

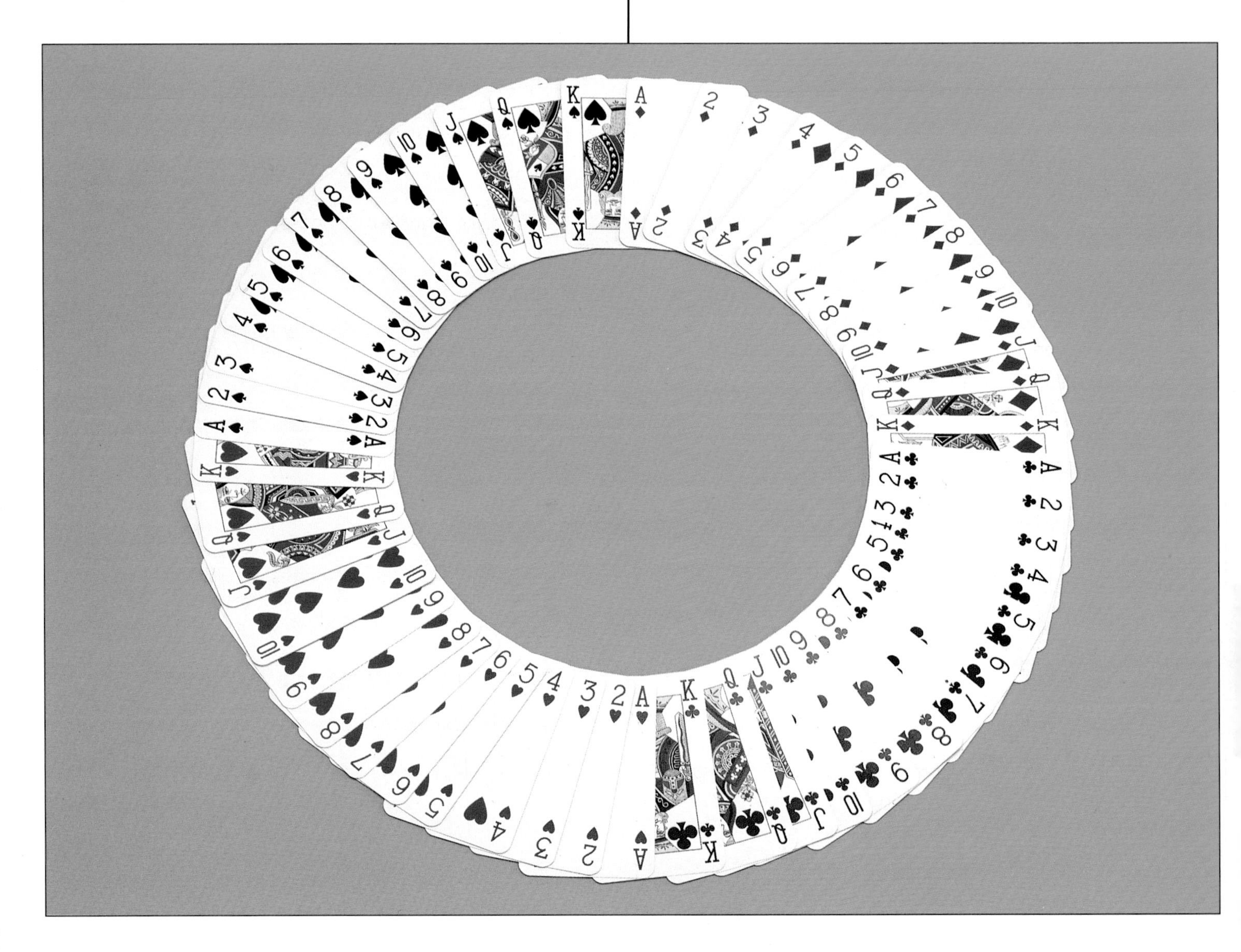

of 364. Add one, representing the deck as a whole, and the answer is 365 – the number of days in the year! Many such numerical parallels with Time and the forces of nature may be drawn and interpreted from the playing cards.

A "single question" system of prediction incorporating a temporal theme links the 52-card deck to 26, a two lunar-year period and offers a method of divination which is both simple and succinct.

PREDICTING BY NUMBERS

List the numbers 1-26 vertically and place by each number the written names of the 52 playing cards in suit order, i.e. Diamonds and Clubs together then Hearts and Spades. In each case, start with an Ace and end with a King (as shown right).

Invite the Enquirer to shuffle the cards thoroughly and to consider his or her question consistently while doing so. Questions such as *"When will I marry?"*; *"Will I start a new job soon?"*; *"When will I meet a new boy/girlfriend?"* can be answered in this way. From a fan of 52 cards, invite the Enquirer to select one (**1**). Find its position on the numbers "ladder". The nearer the card is to the top of the list, the earlier the answer to the Enquirer's question will take place – given that each number represents a time span of one lunar month (28 days). If so required, further interpretation may be given by outlining the meaning of the selected card (see pages 72-79).

1

THE KEY

1	Ace of Diamonds or Clubs
2	Two of Diamonds or Clubs
3	Three of Diamonds or Clubs
4	Four of Diamonds or Clubs
5	Five of Diamonds or Clubs
6	Six of Diamonds or Clubs
7	Seven of Diamonds or Clubs
8	Eight of Diamonds or Clubs
9	Nine of Diamonds or Clubs
10	Ten of Diamonds or Clubs
11	Jack of Diamonds or Clubs
12	Queen of Diamonds or Clubs
13	King of Diamonds or Clubs
14	Ace of Hearts or Spades
15	Two of Hearts or Spades
16	Three of Hearts or Spades
17	Four of Hearts or Spades
18	Five of Hearts or Spades
19	Six of Hearts or Spades
20	Seven of Hearts or Spades
21	Eight of Hearts or Spades
22	Nine of Hearts or Spades
23	Ten of Hearts or Spades
24	Jack of Hearts or Spades
25	Queen of Hearts or Spades
26	King of Hearts or Spades

KEYWORDS TO ALL CARDS AND THEIR REVERSE MEANINGS

DIAMONDS

Ace	Logical reasoning and enthusiasm further personal ambitions.
Reverse	Loss of drive and direction.
King	Ambitious, disciplined, fair-haired man.
Reverse	Devious schemer. Deceptions revealed.
Queen	Strong, independent, fair-haired woman.
Reverse	Spiteful woman. Malicious gossip.
Jack	Intelligent, fair-haired youth or ambitious, immature adult male.
Reverse	Unreliable, stubborn person. Troublemaker.
Ten	Change involving journeys, money or career.
Reverse	Fear of failure brings anxiety.
Nine	New interests ahead. New business venture.
Reverse	Delay. Dispute. Obstacles.
Eight	Career and energy drives blocked.
Reverse	Indecision. Lost opportunities.
Seven	Success in a practical way.
Reverse	Vitality lost. Reassess personal attitudes.
Six	Carefully planned goals are achieved. Caution.
Reverse	Documents mislaid. Information leaked.
Five	Positive action promises future success.
Reverse	Inability to persevere.
Four	Difficult personal decisions necessary.
Reverse	Hasty plans fail.
Three	Practical plans progressed with flair.
Reverse	Lack of drive thwarts ambitions.
Two	Partnerships, business or domestic.
Reverse	Opposition in practical partnerships.

CLUBS

Ace	Determination and enthusiasm bring financial reward.
Reverse	Physical and spiritual poverty.
King	Generous, wealthy, brown-haired man.
Reverse	Miserliness on all levels.
Queen	Intelligent, resourceful, brown-haired woman.
Reverse	Greedy, spiteful woman.
Jack	Enterprising, brown-haired youth or an apathetic adult male.
Reverse	Restlessness. Unreliability. Dishonesty.
Ten	Money from an unexpected source?
Reverse	Spendthrift ways. Despondency.
Nine	Prosperity in all areas.
Reverse	Threat of financial insecurity.
Eight	Financial risks at this time.
Reverse	Control gambling instincts.
Seven	Check money-making plans.
Reverse	Check accounts.
Six	Careful planning and hard work bring rewards.
Reverse	Careless attitude could mean financial ruin.
Five	New directions could bring financial reward.
Reverse	Financial loss through doubtful speculation.

Four	Business relationships. Take special care of personal possessions.
Reverse	Difficulties. Distrust. Delays.
Three	Business and personal fulfilment flourish.
Reverse	Wasted opportunities.
Two	Opposition in joint ventures.
Reverse	Opposition. Spiteful partners.

HEARTS

Ace	Warm, compassionate family feelings. Fertile beginnings.
Reverse	Unsettled home life. Bleakness.
King	Romantic, home-loving, fair-haired man.
Reverse	Indiscretion. Sexual gratification.
Queen	Sensitive, emotional, fair-haired woman.
Reverse	Self-absorption.
Jack	Friendly, immature, fair-haired youth.
Reverse	Unhappy lover, given to self-pity.
Ten	Happiness. Good news concerning family.
Reverse	Family arguments.
Nine	Secret dreams come true.
Reverse	Lovers' enthusiasm misunderstood.
Eight	Joy – or disappointment.
Reverse	Obstacles in romantic affairs.
Seven	Romantic dreams may come true.
Reverse	Disappointment in love.
Six	All is possible – at a price!
Reverse	Self-imposed sacrifice drains energies.
Five	Romantic affairs need careful handling.
Reverse	Opportunities missed.
Four	Unease in family or romantic affairs.
Reverse	Injustice in emotional matters.
Three	Relationships prosper in a fertile way.
Reverse	Exhaustion. Judgement impaired.
Two	Romantic partnerships flourish.
Reverse	Disharmony in romantic relationships.

SPADES

Ace	Caution. Matters erupt and come to a head. New beginnings.
Reverse	Disharmony. Instability. Bad news.
King	Powerful, ruthless, dark-haired man.
Reverse	Unscrupulous dealings. Disruption. Chaos.
Queen	Cunning, hard-hearted, dark-haired woman. Beware.
Reverse	Crafty, spiteful woman who may attack.
Jack	Youthful, dark-haired miscreant or emotionally inadequate adult man.
Reverse	Untrustworthy, treacherous male.
Ten	End of an extremely difficult phase.
Reverse	Matters deteriorate.
Nine	Energies drained. Resources tested.
Reverse	Health problems. Poverty. Rejection.
Eight	Disruptions. Dispute. Deadlock.
Reverse	Persistent misfortune.
Seven	Secret fears. Inner doubts.
Reverse	Malicious, vengeful thoughts.
Six	Set-backs. Disappointments.
Reverse	Ongoing minor disasters.
Five	Miscalculations. Misunderstandings.
Reverse	Unexpected set-backs.
Four	Frustrating deadlocks.
Reverse	Delaying tactics compound troubles.
Three	Third party interference causes disharmony.
Reverse	Broken agreements. Pessimism.
Two	Parting of the ways. Pessimistic feelings followed by optimism for a hopeful outcome.
Reverse	Despair, but hope prevails.

Symbolizing the unknown potential within us all,
the Joker leaps onto the scene with a lively element
of surprise; its presence can be volatile, its effect
illuminating and changeful . . . When the Joker
appears, prepare to expect the unexpected and
meet the challenge as you will!

CONTENTS CHECKLIST

N.B. Several of the divinatory spreads presented in this book were specifically devised by the author. Acknowledged "classic" spreads may have been embellished slightly with additional ritual.